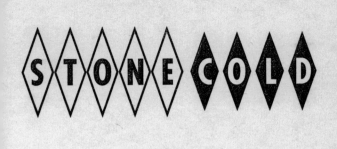

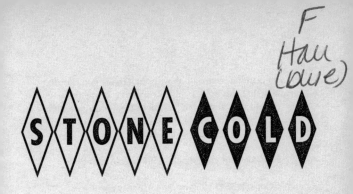

STONE COLD

PETE HAUTMAN

ALADDIN PAPERBACKS
New York London Toronto Sydney Singapore

First Aladdin Paperbacks edition February 2000

Aladdin Paperbacks
An imprint of Simon & Schuster
Children's Publishing Division
1230 Avenue of the Americas
New York, NY 10020

The text for this book was set in Baskerville Book.
Printed and bound in the United States of America.
2 4 6 8 10 9 7 5 3 1

The Library of Congress has cataloged the
hardcover edition as follows:
Hautman, Pete, 1952-
Stone cold / by Pete Hautman.
p.   cm.
Summary: Sixteen-year-old Denn finds himself alienating
both friends and family when he becomes obsessed with
playing high-stakes poker with adult gamblers.
ISBN 0-689-81759-2 (hc.)
[1. Gambling-Fiction. 2. Addiction-Fiction.
3. Poker-Fiction.] I. Title
PZ7.H2887St 1998
[Fic]-dc21
97-48360
ISBN 0-689-83321-0 (pbk.)

FOR M. L. L.

CONTENTS

PART TWO, JULY

PART THREE, AUGUST

PART ONE
JUNE

MR. BUS

It all started the day I got hit by Mr. Bus, but more about that later.

I have a rule. When somebody offers me money, I take it. So when Mrs. Pratt gave me an extra ten bucks for doing a nice job on her lawn, I said, "Thank you very much," and stuck it in my pocket.

I knew what Seamus would say. He'd say, "Denn, Denn, Denn," shaking his head and smiling. Then he'd tell me how Theresa Pratt cut every last coupon out of the paper to save money at the Safeway, and how she never threw away a scrap of tinfoil that could be used again, and how she practically lived on two-day-old bread and generic peanut butter.

I don't know why she gave me the extra ten bucks if she was so hard up.

Actually, Seamus probably wouldn't lecture me, but he'd say something to make me feel guilty, so I didn't mention it when I saw him later that afternoon at St. Luke's. I was trimming around the rosebushes, catching a few rays, when I felt his shadow lay itself across my bare back.

I let go of the trigger on my weed-whacker.

"Hey, Seamus," I said. "How the hell you doing?"

Seamus grinned and shook his head, letting me know that I wasn't going to get a rise out of him that day. I should've known. He was wearing jeans and a T-shirt. When Seamus was out of uniform, you could hardly tell he was a priest.

He said, "I'm doing good, Denn." He gave the garden an appreciative look. "Good job."

"The price was right, that's for sure," I said.

Father Seamus Murray O'Gara laughed. Most people call him Father O'Gara, but I call him Seamus. I like the way it rolls off the tongue: *Shay-muss*. Me and his "sainted mother," he once told me, are the only ones who call him by his first name.

Seamus and I had this deal where I did all the gardening at St. Luke's for free, zippo, nada. In return, Seamus referred some of his parishioners to me. If they could afford it, like Mr. and Mrs. Woodrose, I charged them plenty.

In the real world, nothing is for free.

Seamus might be a priest, but he understands business. He's just like the rest of us, tit for tat, right down to the deals he makes in the confessional. If you're a Catholic you know the drill. Go in the box and say what you did, swap it for a few Hail Marys. Just another transaction.

We talked for a few minutes. That was another thing about Seamus. He was the kind of guy you could hang out with, talk about baseball or rock and roll or whatever, and not have to watch what you say. Except I knew to stay off the subject of old lady Pratt tipping me the tenner. I don't remember what we talked about that day, though. The only reason I remember it at all is because right afterward was when I ran into Mr. Bus.

Rolling down the sidewalk past Manning's Drugs, weed-whacker over my shoulder, I spotted the glint of a quarter on the sidewalk in front of a bus bench. I dropped into a crouch on my skateboard, thinking I'd thread the narrow strip of concrete between the front of the bench and the curb and scoop up the loose cash on the way. I must've lost it at just the wrong moment because the next thing I knew I was flying off the sidewalk into the street. I saw a flash of red and chrome, and something hit my shoulder, spun me around, slammed me back against the bus bench, and flipped my board up into the air. There was a frozen moment then—me lying across the back of the bench, wind knocked out of me, watching everything that was happening, the bus flashing by, the screech of its brakes, a woman's startled face, and my skateboard, higher than the bus, doing its own private airwalk, pausing at the top of its flight, falling back toward me. I reached out one hand and caught it.

The weed-whacker was history, totally mangled by the rear wheels of Mr. Bus.

It was quite a scene after that. The bus driver was the most shook up. He wanted all kinds of information. He got even more upset when I hopped on my board and rolled off with my mangled weed-whacker, but I figured, what do I need the grief for? Nobody got hurt. Except for a little ache in my shoulder, I was feeling good.

Feeling lucky.

JACKS

I tossed the weed-whacker in a dumpster behind the Super Valu. A total write-off. A hundred twenty dollars gone, just like that. I rolled down Girard Street counting money in my head, subtracting the cost of a new weed-whacker from the eleven hundred sixteen dollars in my savings account, adding in the thirty bucks I'd earned that afternoon, plus the ten dollar tip, minus the three fifty I'd spent at Taco Bell for lunch. One thousand thirty-two dollars and change. I wasn't that good in math class, but when it came to money, I could add like a calculator. Sometimes at night if I couldn't sleep I added numbers in my head. I added how much money I could make over the summer, and then tried to figure out how I could come up with the three thousand five hundred dollars that Harold Erickson wanted for his Camaro. On August first I'd be sixteen, eligible for my driver's license. I really wanted that Camaro. It's still possible, I thought. As Murky Stein would say, a *for sure* possibility.

That's what I was thinking about as I rolled past the Hicks place.

"Hey, Doylie!"

My name isn't "Doylie." I hate it when people call me that. My name is Doyle. Dennis Doyle. Denn, if you're my friend. But I knew it was me that was being yelled at, so I looked over and saw Jason Hicks's pink face in the window, grinning at me.

I didn't particularly like Jason, but I didn't particularly dislike him, either. Except when he called me "Doylie." Now that I think about it, I didn't really know him back then.

Jason Hicks was a skinny guy with bugged-out eyes and a lot of red in his face. He had thin blond hair that floated away from his head when the wind blew, and a piercing nasal voice. I usually saw him working at the Franklin Avenue Amoco, or sitting out on his front steps smoking cigarettes. Jason was eigh-teen, I think, but he seemed older. I'd noticed that when kids dropped out of high school they seemed to get old fast.

Jason had dropped out during his senior year and joined the marines. Six months later, he was back home with a discharge. Jason said he got kicked out because he punched out his drill sergeant, but I heard from my mother, who heard it from Jason's aunt, that he'd had a nervous breakdown, and they'd discharged him for being a nut case.

Because we'd grown up on the same street, he usually said "hi" if we ran into each other, but it wasn't like either of us would cross a room to have a conversation. I didn't think about him much, and I don't think he thought much about me. We moved in different circles.

So I was surprised that he'd gone so far as to stick his head out that window and raise his voice to greet me. I thought maybe he wanted me to do some yard work, but I was hot and thirsty, and my weed-whacker was toast. If that was what he wanted, I decided right then and there that I'd say no.

"What's happening?" he asked.

I picked up my board and crossed the lawn to the window. "Nothin' much," I said.

"You busy?"

I shrugged. "Why? You need your weeds whacked?"

Jason thought that was pretty funny, and he let out a high-pitched, squawking laugh. He turned and repeated what I'd said to someone inside. I heard laughter. He leaned out the window again. "You know how to play poker, don't you?" he asked, scratching his thin nose. His fingernails were rimmed with black.

"Why?" I asked. Jason wasn't a scary guy, not what you'd call the violent or criminal type, but I was careful around him. He was older and different from me. I was careful around Seamus, too. For that matter, I was careful around my mom.

"We got a little game going here," he said. "You know how to play, don't you?"

"A little," I said. Poker was one of the things my father, Fred, had shown me before he left. He showed me how to play, then told me not to. He told me, "The less poker you play, the better off you'll be. But if you ever do play, here are some things you should know." Of course, I'd forgotten most of it.

"Why don't you come on in?" he said. "It's cool inside. I got the AC on. You want a beer? The old man's not home."

You know how sometimes a bunch of things come together in life and you make a decision that five minutes earlier you never would've imagined? The way I figure it, it was the combination of hot sun, hard work, almost getting bussed to death, and the way he offered me that beer—like it was the most natural thing in the world. Like I was an adult.

I told myself I'd drink the beer and check out the poker game. I told myself it would be really stupid to gamble, especially with guys who knew how to play the game, but it would be fun to spend a few minutes with some older guys, drinking beer and watching them play cards. At the same time I was telling myself this stuff, I never once forgot about that extra ten bucks from old lady Pratt in my pocket, or the hundred twenty-nine bucks a new weed-whacker was going to cost me, or the fact that I was lucky to be alive. The more I thought about it, the luckier I felt.

This is the part where you maybe think I'm going to tell you that I lost all my money. It could have happened that way. Sometimes I wish it had.

It took about ten minutes for Jason and the other guys—Sam Grant, Tyler Kitterage, and George something-or-other who worked with Jason at the Amoco station—to talk me into playing. Sam and Tyler were both a year older than me, and George looked like he was about thirty. They were betting fifty cents or a dollar at a time, and some of the pots got up to fifteen or twenty bucks. It looked like a lot of money to me. I remember thinking that I'd just try a few hands, and if I lost ten dollars, I'd go home.

The very first hand I was dealt four jacks. I won seven dollars from Ty, who had a straight.

The second hand I won again, with two pair.

The third hand I was dealt a bunch of garbage, something like two, four, nine, jack, king. I bet a dollar anyway, just to see what would happen. Everybody folded and I won the antes.

And I kept winning. After a while, Jason suggested raising the stakes. We upped the limit to two, then three dollars. And I kept right on winning.

I've played a lot of poker since then, but I've never seen cards like the cards I saw that afternoon in Jason Hicks's bedroom. For two hours straight, I could do no wrong. Then Jason's father came home and threw a fit and told Jason if he ever caught him smoking and gambling in the house again he'd be out on the street. He told us all to get the hell out. I didn't care. I was two hundred eighty-seven dollars richer, my pockets bulging with quarters and one-dollar bills, thinking I was hands down the luckiest guy in the world.

Of course, I know now that feeling lucky and being lucky are two totally different things. Sometimes I think that if I'd lost every dime I owned in that first poker game, or if Mr. Bus had rolled on over me instead of just crunching my weed-whacker, I'd have been a lot better off. I mean, maybe *I* wouldn't be better off, but I bet some other people, they'd be a hell of a lot happier with me dead.

FLOWERS

When I was fourteen years old, my father, Frederick Doyle, Jr., went into an advice-giving frenzy. Every day he would tell me three or four new things. He told me to stay in school. He opened a savings account for me with fifty dollars in it, and he told me to always put twenty percent of my earnings in it. He showed me how to change the oil on the car, how to tie a tie, and how to trim the apple tree in the backyard. He showed me how to use the weed-whacker and how to sharpen the lawn mower blade. He showed me all the things he thought were important, and then he left us.

I hated Fred for that. Every day when I missed him I felt these surges of hatred. They only lasted a minute or so, but when they were gone I was left with a sick feeling. I thought of it as a lump of something growing in my belly like a tumor. I hated him most when I needed him for something stupid, like to help me put up a basketball hoop. Or when my mom couldn't open a jar and I had to try to open it but I couldn't get it open either. I hated him when he called from Los Angeles on his speakerphone, dropping all those Hollywood names and bragging about how exciting it was to be in the movie business. He wasn't *in* the movies, he was just another script writer. He'd left Fairview to get into the movie business, sold a couple action-movie scripts, and now he talked like he was Steven Spielberg. I hated that I wanted to talk to him so bad my knees would shake, but when I got on the phone all I could do was be a smart-ass because I was so mad.

Lately, when Fred called, I wouldn't even go near the phone.

But as mad as I was at Fred, I remembered all his advice.

I remembered one day we'd been working on the lawn and Fred got to talking on the subject of women. His style was to rattle things off, as if he were reading from an invisible list. He said, "The older you get, the more you'll like girls.

"When a woman plays with her hair and looks at you, she likes you.

"Never have two girlfriends at the same time.

"When a woman makes you happy, bring her flowers.

"When a woman is unhappy, bring her flowers.

"When she least expects it, bring her flowers."

My father was a jerk for leaving us, but he knew some things.

When Kelly opened her front door and I handed her the bouquet of roses, I knew right away I'd done the right thing. She let out a squeal that hurt my eardrums but left me smiling, then ran back into her house with the roses to show her mother. I followed her into the kitchen, where Mrs. Rollingate was cutting up a chicken.

"My word," she said, looking at the roses. "That's a very nice gift, Dennis."

"Do we have a vase?" Kelly asked.

"Let me look." Mrs. Rollingate rinsed her hands and wiped them on her jeans. The only woman I knew who was tall enough to look me straight in the eye, Mrs. R had long fingers and large teeth to go with her height. Her eyes were black on black. Her hair was pulled back tight into a steel-gray ponytail—it really did look like a pony's tail—that hung most of the way down her back. When she spoke, the words came out slow, like she was thinking about each one separately. Kelly told me her mom had been a model back in the 1970s.

Kelly was the opposite of her mother. She was short, slightly plump, and she had small sky-colored eyes that slanted up, kind of like a Siamese cat. She had full lips that always looked ready to kiss, a scatter of freckles across her nose, and reddish-blond hair that never did what she wanted but always looked great to me.

Unlike her mother, who never got excited about anything, Kelly got excited about *everything*. For her, life was one dramatic event after another. I liked being around her impulsive energy, even when it drove me nuts, and I liked looking at her. We were boyfriend and girlfriend, but we were also *friends*. I'd known Kelly since the eighth grade.

Mrs. Rollingate climbed up on a stool to get a vase from one of the kitchen cabinets. As soon as she turned her back, Kelly gave me a surprise kiss.

"I heard that," said Mrs. Rollingate. Kelly laughed, and I blushed. Mrs. R climbed down with a tall glass vase. "You have to cut the ends off the stems and put them in warm water," she told Kelly.

As Kelly used a kitchen shears on the rose

stems, her mother poured me a glass of cranberry juice. We sat down at the kitchen table. "Roses are very expensive," she said to me. "Your gardening business must be doing well."

"I'm doing okay," I admitted. The roses had only cost me eight dollars. I bought all my landscaping supplies from the people at Lunden Nursery, so they gave me a deal on the flowers.

"Ouch!" said Kelly.

"Be careful of the thorns," warned Mrs. Rollingate. She gave me a peculiar smile. "I was twenty years old the first time a man gave me roses," she mused.

I drank my juice.

"You kids grow up so fast these days," she continued. "Sometimes I wish you'd slow down."

I nodded, thinking about how I had to do all the things Fred used to do. In some ways I wouldn't have minded being a kid for a while longer.

Mrs. Rollingate had her black eyes fixed on me. "I like you, Dennis."

"Uh, thank you," I said, embarrassed.

"That's not a compliment," she said. "It's a simple fact. I hope I still like you five years from now. You're how old now?"

"Sixteen this August."

She shook her head and said quietly, "You could be anybody. You could be the nicest man in the world, or you could become a heartless jerk."

"That won't happen," I said.

Mrs. Rollingate sighed and smiled and pressed her long fingers against her temples. "I know it won't, Dennis. You shouldn't listen to me."

Kelly plunked the vase full of roses down between us. "Ta-da!" she said.

Mrs. Rollingate said, "They are quite beautiful, dear." She stood up. "I'm going to lie down for a while." She pointed at the cut-up chicken on the counter. "Would you please put that away for me, dear?"

After she'd left the room, Kelly said to me, "My mom gets kinda weird sometimes."

"So does mine," I said.

SWANS

On the way home from Kelly's I stopped at the bank and put $150 in my savings account, bringing it up to $1,266. I still had $165 in my pocket, enough to replace my weed-whacker and then some. I went to Riverside Mall and treated myself to a huge, sticky cinnamon roll from Cinnabon. Giving the roses to Kelly had put me in a gift-buying mood. I bought a small silver pin shaped like a pair of swans from The Booty Boutique. The swans cost $26, but I knew my mom would like it. No one had bought her a present in a long time.

Mom had this thing about swans. She had swan knickknacks, swan dish towels, and a ceramic swan planter overflowing with ivy. She had a black T-shirt with white swans on the front, and a painting of a pair of sleeping swans in her bedroom. She even had salt-and-pepper shakers shaped like swans. Actually, they looked more like geese, but she called them swans. As far as I knew, she didn't have a silver swan pin.

I was right again. She went nuts over it, kissing and hugging me about twenty times, which was nineteen times too many hugs and kisses for my taste.

My mother, Sally Doyle, was always way too nice to me. She never let me do anything around the house, except for yard work and opening pickle jars. She treated me like I was a prince or something, like she was afraid if she said or did the wrong thing, I'd have her beheaded. It was embarrassing. Every morning she got up and made me breakfast, and she made sure I had lots of clean clothes, and she would drive me anyplace I wanted to go, anytime. Since my father had left us, she just didn't have enough to do. She talked about going back to school, or doing volunteer work, or even getting a real job, but she never seemed to get around to it. Once a month she got a check for $2,300 from Fred, so money wasn't a huge problem. That was another thing that made me mad. If she'd had to get a job, I think she might've been happier. In a way, my father's checks kept her trapped at home, doing nothing.

Of course, if he hadn't sent us the money I'd have hated him worse.

She put the pin on her blouse right away and admired it in the hall mirror.

My mother was a beautiful woman, and I'm not just saying that. At thirty-eight, she was much prettier than Kelly's mom, the ex-model. She had lots of light brown hair and the biggest, friendliest smile you can imagine. She never did any exercise except housework, but she had stayed slim and young looking. Sometimes when we were out in public, people would think we were brother and sister. I had seen the way older men looked at her. She'd been asked out on dates a few times, but she always turned them down flat. A few months ago, Bob Stockman, who owned Big Bob's Sports Emporium, had invited her to a Neil Diamond concert. I overheard her tell him she had other plans. I knew that wasn't true, so I asked her why she didn't want to go to the concert. Neil Diamond was one of her favorites.

She told me she wasn't ready to start dating. "You're man enough for me, Denn," she said, making it a joke.

That had made me uncomfortable, like I was this huge drag on her social life. At the same time, I knew I had nothing to do with it. She actually thought that someday Fred would come back to us.

"It's a beautiful pin, Denn," she said, turning back and forth to watch it catch the light. "Did you know that swans mate for life?"

Yeah, I knew. She'd only told me that about five hundred times before.

COOKIES

Murky said, "This is *so* cool!"

Murky thought everything was cool. You could show him a particularly large zit and he would say, "That is *so* cool!"

I said, "It's a lawn mower, Murk."

"Man, I bet it'd mow *anything*." He twisted the steering wheel back and forth, making engine sounds with his mouth.

"Yeah, it probably would," I said, edging away. Murky, better known to teachers and strangers as Mark Stein, could be kind of embarrassing to be with, even in the lawn and garden department of Sears. He was sort of fat and sort of sloppy and he always blurted out whatever popped into his head.

When we were alone together he could be really funny. In fact, Murky was hands down the funniest kid I ever met. He could make a dog laugh. But the same things that made him funny in private made him a total embarrassment to be with in public. One time he painted a cane white and walked around all afternoon in downtown Fairview pretending to be blind. That sort of stuff was getting old. A couple years ago, when we were in junior high, it hadn't been such a big deal. People expect kids to act stupid. But now, pretending to drive a riding lawn mower at Sears, stuff like that just wasn't as funny anymore.

I headed for the edgers and trimmers. After buying my mom that swan pin the day before, and then playing some video games with Murky and eating lunch at the B. K., I had exactly $131.49 in my pocket. The last weed-whacker I'd bought had cost $119.99 plus tax, so I figured I had just enough money to cover it.

Wouldn't you know. The price had gone up to $129.99. Plus tax.

I could've bought one of the cheaper models, but once you get used to a good weed-whacker, you don't want to lower your standards. I remembered Fred telling me how to buy tools. "Pay for quality," he'd said.

I was standing there staring at the row of trimmers and edgers when Murky came up and said, "Hey, weed-whackers. Cool!" He grabbed the one I'd been looking at, pointed it at me, and started making weed-whacking noises.

"C'mon, let's go," I said.

"Where we going?"

"To the bank. I have to get some more money out," I said, walking away.

Murky replaced the whacker and caught up with me. We were halfway across the mall when Murky said he had to go to the bathroom. I knew what that meant. The rest rooms were up by the food court.

"I'm not spending any more money," I said.

"What are you talking about? I thought you were this big poker hero. Mr. Moneybags. Beat Jason Hicks out of his inheritance or something. Denny 'Sagebrush Slim' Doyle, the gamblin' man." He started singing. *"You got to fold when you hold 'em . . . "*

"That's not how it goes."

". . . know when you're moldy . . . "

I took off my cap and slapped him on the back of the head to shut him up. We both started laughing.

"Now I really got to go to the bathroom," he said, walking faster.

"Okay, but I'm not gonna spend what I've got on food. I don't even have enough on me to buy a new whacker." I really hated taking money out of the bank.

Murky shrugged and rubbed the shaggy

back of his head. "That's okay, I got money."

"You do? Then how come you let me buy you lunch?"

"So I'd have enough left to buy us dessert. Whaddya say, Sagebrush Slim? How 'bout we head over to the cookie corral and rope us a couple a them chocolate-chip disks, pardner?"

Murky's humor had a tendency to wander off. Somehow my winning at poker had, in his mind, made me into a cowboy. He'd be doing his lousy impression of John Wayne for hours.

The cookie joint in the food court makes cookies the size of a Frisbee. I could eat a whole one, but not all at one sitting, so after Murky finished his peanut butter cookie, he got started on the last half of my chocolate chip.

Murky was telling me a funny story about his bar mitzvah, still with the John Wayne accent, spraying cookie crumbs all over the table, when he saw something behind me and clammed up. I turned around. It was Jason Hicks and Gibby Newhouse, walking straight toward us.

"Hey there, Doylie!" Jason's voice was in full nasality.

"Hi, Jason."

He took up a position behind my left

shoulder, so I had to twist my neck uncomfortably to look up at him.

"Spend all your winnings yet?"

"Not yet," I said.

Jason turned to Gibby. "You shoulda seen the hands this guy got yesterday. Like he couldn't lose."

Gibby gave me and Murky a wordless, expressionless look—not a mean or threatening stare, but more the way you might look at somebody's little brother. Like we weren't quite alive.

I mentioned before that Jason didn't scare me. He was a lot of bark and not much bite. But Gibby Newhouse, he was genuinely scary.

Gibby stood about five foot eight, a couple inches shorter than me. He couldn't've weighed more than one-thirty, and he wore wire-rimmed glasses. His face was pointy, like a Doberman pinscher, with small, dark eyes and a narrow-lipped mouth always hung open so you could see his crooked front tooth. Gibby didn't look like your typical tough guy, but he was afraid of nothing and nobody, and he had a temper like a rabid skunk. Gibby Newhouse did not care if he got hurt—it just flat-out did not matter to him. I once saw him get in a fight with John Beal, the biggest guy on the football team, in the school lunchroom. I don't know what started it. All of a sudden Gibby was all over Beal, kicking and gouging and fighting so fast and dirty that Beal never knew what hit him. Beal was sidelined with a bandage over his eye for nearly a month. Gibby got suspended, but that was okay with him. I think that might've been the whole point of it. He never returned to school to finish his senior year.

"So, what're you up to?" Jason asked me.

"He's shopping for a new weed-whacker," Murky blurted.

For some reason, Jason thought that was pretty funny and let loose his squawk of a laugh. Gibby's little black eyes blinked suspiciously at Murky, looking for hidden insults or mockery. Murky shrank into his seat and pushed the rest of my cookie into his mouth.

I said, "My weed-whacker broke."

"So what do you say you give me a chance to win my money back?" Jason suggested.

"Here?"

"Nah. At my house. Ty and Sam are coming over in about half an hour. Gibby, he wants to play, don't you Gibb?"

Gibby shrugged. "Sure."

"Then we got a game," Jason said.

I said, "I thought your dad told you no more poker."

"He's in Chicago till Friday. Whaddya say?"

"I don't know. I don't think I can afford it."

"I know you got money, Doylie. C'mon, give us a chance. It's only fair. Besides, maybe you'll win again. Buy yourself a whole garage full of weed-whackers."

The image of a garage full of weed-whackers did not appeal to me.

"No thanks," I said. "I just don't feel lucky today."

I don't remember how Jason convinced me to play. Maybe it was nothing he'd said; maybe it was something inside of me. Whatever. I was back in Jason Hicks's bedroom, sitting on the floor playing poker again, only this time the cards weren't cooperating.

"Five more," Gibby said, throwing a five-dollar bill in the pot.

I looked at my cards again. A pair of aces. Murky was hanging over my shoulder, filling the air with stale peanut butter breath. I gave him an elbow, and he backed off. Sam Grant was lying on Jason's bed wearing his Walkman, his feet quivering to an unheard beat. He had busted out on the first three hands. Ty and Jason had already dropped out of the hand. It was just me and Gibby Newhouse.

"You in or not?" he asked.

A pair of aces. Was that good enough to call a five-dollar bet? Gibby was staring at me hard, his beady eyes practically giving me sunburn. I looked at the small pile of money in front of me, less than fifty dollars left of the hundred and thirty-one I'd started with. I took one more look at Gibby's face, then threw my cards down.

"Take it," I said. "I fold."

Gibby grinned—a truly scary sight with all those little teeth—and showed me his cards. A pair of threes. He'd bluffed me. I felt sick.

Behind me, Murky said, "I knew he was bluffing."

"Shut up," I said. We'd been playing for hours. I was in no mood to be second-guessed by Murky.

I was tired and hungry, but I kept wanting to play the next hand. One more hand.

Jason said, "I once saw a guy at Marcel's get bluffed out of two thousand dollars."

"What's Marcel's?" Murky asked.

"That fancy restaurant down by the river," I said. "My dad used to take my mom there."

"There's a big game there every weekend,"

Jason said. "Guys lose their paychecks. Guys win thousands. It's the biggest game in town."

"How do you know?" I asked.

"I work there."

"Thought you worked at the Amoco."

"That's my day job. I work three nights a week at Marcel's."

"Doing what?"

"I'm a manager."

Gibby laughed. "You manage to clean the toilets."

Jason told him to go stick his head in the toilet and see how clean it was. That didn't make much sense, but everybody laughed.

"Five-card draw," said Ty, dealing the cards.

One more hand.

POPCORN

The next morning at nine o'clock I withdrew $266 from my bank account, bringing it down to $1,000 even. I walked to Sears, paid $139.08 including tax for a new weed-whacker, and then delivered $125 to Gibby Newhouse, who lived with his sister in an apartment up on Twentieth.

I must've woke him up. He answered the door in his underwear, rubbing his eyes, took the money without comment, gave me back my IOU and closed the door.

I went home, pushed my Toro over to the Fredericksons', and mowed their lawn. Then I trimmed Mrs. Powers's spirea bushes, which had finally dropped their blossoms.

And all morning, I kept thinking about that poker game. I had lost more than $250. Lost it so fast, it seemed unreal, one hand after another. Then I remembered something Fred had told me. He'd said, "Poker isn't a game of chance. It's a game of skill. No matter how lucky you get, a skillful card player will win your money in the end."

Was Gibby Newhouse a skillful card player? Maybe.

Was he smarter than me?

I didn't think so. But he had two things I was lacking: experience and knowledge. Experience would take time. But knowledge, that was something I could lay my hands on right away.

The downtown library had a whole shelf of books about poker. I checked out three: *Poker Theory*, *Poker for Idiots*, and *Mike Caro's Book of Tells*. When I got home I started right in on *Poker for Idiots*. When Murky showed up at my house that afternoon, I was sitting cross-legged on my bed dealing poker hands to imaginary players.

"Playing solitaire?" Murky asked.

"Sort of." I showed him *Poker for Idiots*. "I'm trying to figure out what I did wrong yesterday."

Murky looked at the book and laughed. "You sure got the right book." When I didn't laugh, he asked, "Figure anything out yet?"

"Yeah, a couple things. Like, don't bet a four-card straight unless you've got a chance to get five times your money back if you draw the right card."

Murky said, "Huh?" Murky didn't have the kind of brain that could wrap itself around that. He said, "You ask me, there's only two things you need to know about poker."

"Like what?"

"Like, don't let a guy bluff you. And if you have a pair of jacks or better, always stay in. *For sure.*"

Now it was my turn to laugh.

Murky said, "Hey, I'm not the one that lost two hundred fifty bucks yesterday."

"Yeah, you'd have lost twice that."

"Well, I didn't, and I wouldn't have. I coulda made some money off those guys." He jingled some change in his pocket. "You want to go over to Pop's? I raided the ol' piggy bank."

"Nah. I'm not in the mood to throw away any more money."

"My treat. I've got eight bucks here."

"I think I'll stay home," I said. "I'm kinda tired. Besides, I'm not so much into the video games anymore. They're all the same." I gathered up the cards on my bedspread and shuffled them, waiting for Murk to leave.

He said, "You want to go bowling, then?"

"*Bowling*? Are you kidding me?"

"It was just an idea."

"Yeah, a really stupid idea." I could see that stung him, but I didn't care. I'd had enough of Mark Stein on that particular afternoon. I said, "I just don't feel like doing anything, okay?"

I started dealing hands to my imaginary players. After a few minutes, Murky went away.

"Here's how it works," I said. "A guy raises you ten dollars and he's staring right at your face. What does that mean?"

Kelly said, "I don't know. He thinks you're cute?"

"It means he's bluffing."

"Oh." She picked an old maid from the popcorn bowl, crunched it between her teeth. We were sitting in the kitchen. Her mom was in the family room watching *The Tonight Show*.

"It's called a *tell*," I explained. "If you know what to look for, you can *tell* what people are going to do. Little things, like if a guy counts out a bunch of extra chips and holds them in his hand like he's going to raise, it means he's really hoping that you don't bet. He's trying to scare you off."

"That's really interesting, Denn."

"This book I got, the *Book of Tells*, it's full

of stuff like that. It's really cool, almost like mind reading."

"Are you going to play with those guys again, Denn?"

"I don't know. But if I do, I'll know what to look for."

"I don't like them," Kelly said. "That Jason, he creeps me out."

"He's okay. He just likes to act tough."

"Uh-huh." Kelly yawned, covering her mouth with her hand, then grinned. "Was that a tell?" She had a little piece of popcorn hull stuck between her front teeth.

"I think so," I said, standing up to leave. "You want to do something Saturday?"

Kelly tipped her head. "Sure. What?"

"I'll call you."

I stayed up till four in the morning reading the poker books and dealing hands to imaginary players. The more I read, the more I understood. It was like reading books filled with magic spells, only these spells were real. My imaginary players took on identities. Jason. Gibby. Tyler. Sam. Me. I could almost see them sitting around my bed. I could almost smell Jason's cigarettes.

PROUD

I felt bad about being a jerk to Murky, so the next afternoon I called him up and we went down to Pop's Arcade to waste some money. We weren't there ten minutes when Sam Grant showed up.

"Hey, Denn, Jason's been looking for you."

"He couldn't have looked very hard. I was home all morning."

"Yeah, well, anyways, his old man's out of town till Saturday and he's trying to get up a game for tonight."

I opened my mouth to say I wasn't interested, but what came out was, "What time?"

"He's got to work till seven. Gibby and me, we're going over there about eight."

"Who else is playing?"

"I don't know. Ty's broke. You know anybody else might want to play?"

I shook my head.

Then Murky said, "Hey, what about me?"

* * *

At dinner that night, Mom told me that Fred had called.

"We talked for the longest time," she said. "He's so proud of you, Denn. Running your own landscaping business and everything."

"I just mow a few lawns. It's no big deal." I shoveled a load of spaghetti into my mouth, sopped up the last of the sauce with a chunk of bread and loaded that in too.

"And in two more years you'll have graduated from high school. I just can't believe how time flies. It seems like just last week that your father and I got married."

"It seems like just last week you got divorced," I said through a mouthful of bread and pasta.

That shut her up. She moved the noodles around on her plate and ate a couple small bites without saying anything. Finally she said, "He wants you to call him."

I chewed for a while, then swallowed. "What for?"

"You're his son. He wants to talk to you."

"Yeah, right."

"He said you should call him collect."

"He's so generous." I stood up and carried my plate to the sink.

"I'll do the dishes, Denn. I think you

should call your father."

"I'd rather wash dishes."

"Denn!"

"Okay, all right." I grabbed the cordless phone and dialed a number.

Murky answered the phone.

I said, "Hi, Dad."

Murky said, "Huh?"

"Hold on a sec." I walked the phone into my bedroom and closed the door.

"Gee, Dad, it's sure great to talk to you, you flaming asshole."

"Denn? Is that you?"

"Yeah, it's me. Who do you think?"

"I dunno. Some insane foaming-at-the-mouth lunatic?"

"I'm supposed to be calling Fred. So, any-ways, you still think you want to play cards with these guys tonight?"

"Sure. Why not?"

"I already told you why not, but I don't suppose it'll help if I say it again."

"Probably not."

"I'll stop by in a half hour or so, we can walk over together. See you then."

I hung up, stared at my Metallica poster for about five minutes, then opened up the *Book of Tells* and paged through it slowly, fixing the details in my mind.

On the way out the door, my mom asked me what Fred had had to say.

"Not much," I told her. "I did most of the talking."

TELLS

"Hey hey hey, it's the Lawnboy Kid and his faithful sidekick Monkey! C'mon in!"

I didn't have to see the empties to know that Jason had drunk a few beers. We followed him into the kitchen, where Gibby and Sam were sitting at the table. Gibby was shuffling a deck of cards, and Sam was reading one of Mr. Hicks's *Playboy*s.

Gibby said, "Now we got a game."

Jason opened the refrigerator and pulled out a couple cans of Budweiser. "Want a beer?" he asked.

"Not for me," I said. One of the first things I'd read in *Poker for Idiots* was don't drink while playing cards.

Jason held out one of the cans to Murky. To my surprise, Murky took it, popped it open, and took a sip. I'd never seen Murky drink.

We sat down at the table, and everybody

pulled out their money. I had forty-four dollars. I'd decided that if I lost it, I'd quit. Murky surprised me again by putting five twenty-dollar bills on the table. I'd never seen him with that much money. The Murky I knew was always broke. We all anted a quarter, and Gibby dealt a hand of five-card draw.

Sam, sitting on my right, bet a dollar.

I looked at my cards. I had a pair of eights, a ten, a jack, and a queen. If I stayed in I could throw away one of the eights and hope to draw a nine. That would give me a straight. But according to *Poker for Idiots*, the chances that I'd actually get that nine were only one in twelve And even if I did get it, I still might lose to a better hand like a flush or a full house.

"I fold," I said. I'd wait for a better hand to risk my money.

"Raise a buck," said Jason, throwing out two bills with a drunken flourish.

Murky frowned at his cards, then looked at his money. "I raise three more," he said.

Gibby folded. Sam and Jason covered the raises, and they all drew cards. Sam and Jason both drew three.

Murky said, "I'll take five."

"You can't do that," said Jason.

"Why not?"

"Nobody draws five cards."

"Nobody said I couldn't."

Sam said, "Hey, let him draw five. What's the difference?"

"Okay, but from now on nobody gets to draw more than three. House rules."

Gibby gave Murky five new cards.

Murky said, "I bet five dollars."

"You can't bet five. The limit's three."

"Okay then, I bet three."

"I call," said Sam, adding his money to the pot.

"I call, too," said Jason. "Let's see what you got, Monkey."

"My name's Mark. And I got five hearts." He laid his cards on the table.

I thought Jason's eyes were going to pop right out of his head. "You got a *flush*? You drew *five cards* and you got a *flush*?"

"That's why they call it poker," said Murky, raking in the money.

For the next half hour, Murky dominated the game. He won the next seven hands without missing a bet. When he got called, he had the best hand. And when everybody else folded, it turned out Murky was bluffing. Jason was down more than fifty dollars. Sam was down thirty, and Gibby had lost more than both of them put together. It reminded me of my first game. It didn't matter that the Murkster didn't know what he was doing. The cards loved him.

As for me, I was holding even, waiting for the right cards to come along. And while I waited, I studied the opposition, looking for tells.

I found plenty.

When Jason looked at his cards and then lit a cigarette, he usually had a good hand. Sam Grant sat up a little straighter when he liked his cards. Gibby made it a point to look bored. If he looked bored and then raised, he always had winners.

But Murky was the most obvious. When Murky had a lousy hand, he cleared his throat. When he had a good hand, he licked his lips a lot. When he was about to bluff he'd always lean forward, his chest touching the edge of the table. I was amazed that nobody else seemed to notice.

And then, the worm turned.

The basic strategy of poker is simple. When you think you have the best hand, you try to get as much money into the pot as possible. You bet and raise and try to get the other players to throw their money in, too. And when your cards are lousy, you fold and wait for the next hand.

Murky had a different idea. When his cards were good, he bet. And when his cards were bad, he bet then, too. He wanted to win every pot. It had worked for the first few hands, but suddenly his luck deserted him. He and Gibby started going head-to-head on a hand of five-card draw, raising each other repeatedly. Murky was pushing his chest against the table and clearing his throat repeatedly. Gibby, looking bored, kept raising. There must've been a hundred dollars in the pot when a shadow passed across Murky's face, and instead of raising again he said, "I call."

Murky had a pair of threes.

Gibby had a pair of kings.

As Gibby raked in the pot, he said, "I knew you was bluffing, Monkey."

After that, things didn't go so good for poor Murk. Gibby had him figured out, and the dumb luck that had carried Murky that first half hour had gone away. He stayed in every hand, no matter how lousy his cards were. And every hand, he lost.

As for me, I started to rake in the money. I could read the other players so accurately, it was like they were showing me their cards. Every little mannerism meant something. The way they held their cards. The way they sat in their chairs. The little tics and tremors that appeared on their faces. When Sam sorted his cards a certain way, I could tell he had a pair. When he yawned, pretending to be bored, it meant he expected to win the pot. I watched their eyes. Jason's pupils would get bigger when he liked his cards. When he was ner-vous about a hand, his pupils would shrink, as if a bright light were shining on him. Gibby liked to squint at his cards. When they were no good, he would close his eyes completely and look again, as if hoping the cards would change. Little clues, but when I added them all up it was like mind reading.

Murky, it didn't even matter what he had. After losing that big hand to Gibby, he started playing so stupid, I was embarrassed for him. It took him less than an hour to throw away all the money he'd won, plus money he'd brought with him.

"Hey, Denn, how 'bout a little loaner," he said. "Twenty bucks. I'll pay you back next week."

"You sure, Murk? You'll just lose it."

I figured I was doing him a favor by being

blunt, but I could see I'd embarrassed him. I guess it was pretty cruel of me to say it like that in front of the other guys, but hey, I hadn't asked him to play. In fact, I'd tried to discourage it.

"You gonna loan me or not?" he said.

I sailed a twenty across the table. Murky snatched it up.

"Thanks," he said.

The next hand, I caught trip aces and won that twenty dollars, plus sixteen more. Murky stood up and left without a word. As soon as the door closed behind him, Gibby started laughing.

"What a fish!" he crowed. "Do you believe that guy? We gotta get him back here again. Talk about your easy money!"

Jason and Sam were laughing, too.

I said, "Hey, give the guy a break. He's never played before."

"Yeah? Well he's still a dumb-ass."

I pushed the deck toward Jason. "Deal the cards. Come on. Let's play some poker."

Jason scooped up the deck, but before he could shuffle them, the phone rang. He got up and answered it. I heard him say, "Hello?" and then silence.

After a few seconds we all turned to look at him. He was holding the phone to his ear.

His face had gone dead white, and his pupils were constricted to tiny black dots on disks of pale blue. I could hear a faint voice, like a dog growling, coming over the phone. Jason nodded, cleared his throat, then said, "Okay. I will. I promise." He listened to the dog-growl some more. "Okay. No problem. I'll have it Monday. You don't have to worry about me. I—"

He licked his lips, looked at the phone, hung it up, then looked at us with an odd expression, as if he was surprised to find three guys playing cards in his kitchen. It only took him a second to clap his hands together and say, with false heartiness, "Let's play us some poker, gentlemen!"

Nobody asked Jason who had called. I had the feeling that Gibby and Sam knew. Whoever it was, Jason was really shook. He started playing as bad as Murky, trying to win every pot, giving his money away as fast as he could, a desperate gleam in his frightened eyes.

It took me an hour to clean them all out. I walked home with nearly four hundred dollars in my pockets.

DEAD

It was after eleven when I got home, but I called Kelly anyway. She answered the phone in a sleepy voice.

"I just won four hundred dollars," I said.

"Denn?"

"You should've seen me, Kell. I knew what everybody had. They never had a chance. I could read them like I had X-ray vision. He's bluffing. He's got a good hand. He's got two pair. He's drawing to a flush. You know what I think, Kell? I think I have a talent." I emptied my pockets onto my bed, then plopped down on top of all that money.

"You . . . what? Denn, you're not making sense. You were playing poker again?"

"I'm good at it, Kell. Maybe I should be a professional gambler."

"Now you're being silly."

"I'm serious, Kell. I think I have the talent."

"Denn . . . how much did you say you won?"

"Almost four hundred dollars. I'm gonna take you someplace real nice for your birthday." Kelly's golden birthday was coming up—she'd be sixteen on July sixteenth. "Someplace fancy."

"Like where?"

A name popped into my head. "How about Marcel's?"

I tried to call Murky. Mrs. Stein answered.

"Isn't it a little late to be calling?" she asked.

I told her I was sorry, but I wasn't really. Murk had told me that his mother never went to bed before two in the morning. She stayed up and watched the shopping channels.

A few seconds later Murky got on the phone. I told him how the game had ended up, told him about the last hand when I'd wiped out Jason and Gibby with a pair of queens.

"You won how much?" he asked.

"Three hundred and sixty-three dollars."

"That's great, Denn."

He didn't sound all that happy for me. I shouldn't have been surprised. I'd embarrassed him in front of Jason and Gibby and

Sam. But it was his own fault for being such a lousy poker player. My philosophy was if you can't do something well, then you shouldn't be doing it at all. Take me, for instance. I can't sing, so I don't. People appreciate that.

But I didn't say any of that to Murky.

I said, "I guess I got lucky." There was something I'd been wondering about. I didn't know how to ask it, so I just blurted it out. "Hey, Murk? Where'd you get all that money you brought?"

He didn't answer right away. Then he said, "It was from my bar mitzvah."

It took me hours to fall asleep that night. I kept thinking about that stupid Murky digging into the money he'd gotten for his bar mitzvah, the $2,400 that he'd sworn never to touch until he needed it to help pay for college. If his mom found out he'd lost a chunk of it at a poker game, Murky would be jerky. Dead meat.

My thoughts drifted back to the game. Murky had played terrible, but I had played great. I remembered the feeling of power. The feeling of being in control, of reading the other players. When I finally drifted to sleep I dreamed of cards and money and faces. I dreamed that Jason's face was a mirror, and that Sam Grant's fingers were made of wood. Gibby was dark and scary, and Murky had on a clown nose. When my mom woke me up it was nine-thirty and the sun was pouring across my bed. She handed me the phone.

I sat up and cleared my throat, still pretty much unconscious. "Hello?"

"Hey there, sport! Good morning!"

I winced. The voice was too loud and too cheerful, and it was my father. I flopped back onto my bed.

"Hi, Fred."

"Sleeping in this morning, eh?"

My mother gave me a little wave and backed out the door.

"That's right," I said.

"So! I hear you've got your own landscaping business!"

"I'm mowing lawns for some people, that's all."

"You mother tells me you're saving up to buy a car. You turn sixteen this year! That's great!"

"Yeah, well, so, how are you doing?"

"Great! Really, really good, Denn. You've got to come out here and see me sometime. What d'you say? Spend a week with the old man?"

"Um. I dunno. I'm pretty busy. You know, with my landscaping business."

"I thought you were just mowing a few lawns!" He laughed. "What about later this month? I'll send you a plane ticket. You can fly out for a few days, check out the California lifestyle. I'll give you a tour of the studios, maybe introduce you to some movie stars."

I said, "Y'know, Fred, I'm kinda half asleep here. Can I call you back?"

The second time I woke up it was almost noon and my mother was gone. She left a note saying she had gone to an Audubon Society meeting. My mother liked to talk about birds, but that was her problem. My problem was breakfast. I decided to make myself some pancakes.

I only know how to cook a few things, but I like to do it right. I make my pancakes from scratch. A cup of flour, some baking powder, a handful of sugar, and a dash of salt. Add a cup of buttermilk, one or two eggs, a couple tablespoons of oil, then stir. That's all there is to it. I was feeling reckless, so I chopped up some strawberries and threw those in, too. Then I heated up the Teflon skillet and poured myself a big one. I don't believe in wimpy pancakes.

If it's not at least ten inches across it's not a serious pancake.

My recipe makes two serious pancakes. Halfway through the second one the phone started ringing. I let the answering machine pick up. It was Fred again, asking me to call. I let him leave his message, then finished eating.

I thought about Murky. His dad had died from a heart attack when we were in the seventh grade. In a weird way, I envied him.

I left the dishes in the sink so my mother would have something to do when she got home. Me, I had to catch up on my work for Seamus. On the way out of the house I erased Fred's message.

I walked the Toro and my new weed-whacker over to St. Luke's to mow the cemetery behind the rectory. It's not much of a cemetery—only about thirty headstones. The most recent one belongs to Eleanor Swenson, who died in 1939. I guess after that they ran out of room.

I stood there looking out over those tombstones sticking up out of the four-inch-tall grass. It's a hassle to mow and trim around all those stones. I suddenly felt tired. Maybe I'd had too much sleep. I did not want to start that mower. Four inches, six inches, what's the difference? I turned around and wheeled the mower toward home without cutting a blade of cemetery grass. Nobody knows any of the dead people there anyways.

MR. CIGAR

Since I'd won all their money, I didn't expect to hear from Jason and Company for a while, but I was wrong. They wanted to play again the next night.

I walked over to Jason's after dinner. Jason and Gibby and Sam were sitting out on his front steps. As soon as they saw me coming, they piled into Gibby's old Dodge and drove down the street to meet me.

"Hop in," Gibby said.

I got in back with Sam. "Where we going?"

"Doughboy's. His mom's out of town, so he said we could play at her place."

I knew who Doughboy was, but I'd never actually talked to him. He was a couple years older than Jason and Sam. He and his mother ran a newsstand outside the Palmer Building.

We drove a few miles south to Lake

Eastwood Estates, out near the airport. Lake Eastwood is not really a lake. It's an overgrown little pond choked with cattails and ripe with the smell of rotting vegetation. And the "Estates" were not really estates, but a motley collection of mobile homes set on concrete slabs. A lot of them had old tires strapped on top to keep the roofs from lifting off during a windstorm. Doughboy's mom's trailer was one of the nicer ones. Her tires were whitewalls.

"Doughboy's a pig, but he always loses," Sam whispered to me as we entered the mobile home.

Doughboy sat shuffling cards at a round card table that filled one end of the trailer. He wasn't quite as white as the Pillsbury Doughboy, but more the color of pancake batter. A large plastic salad bowl full of corn chips was wedged between his belly and the edge of the card table.

"You're late," he said, his mouth full of chips. Doughboy had so much face that his eyes looked like little black slits.

Thirty seconds later we were playing cards. I sat down between Doughboy and Jason. Big mistake. Doughboy was constantly scratching himself and belching and farting and digging fistfuls of corn chips from the bowl in his lap. He would bet on anything, and Jason would raise him every time.

Between avoiding Doughboy's elbow and trying not to breathe in his farts and listening to him crunching chips and Jason chain-smoking Marlboros and cackling in my other ear every time he won a pot, I was so distracted that I lost about fifty bucks in the first hour. Sam had put his headphones on and was beating out a tune by rapping his knuckles on the edge of the table. We were playing these strange wild-card games that didn't make any sense—games like "Follow the Queen" and "Night Baseball." Jason and Gibby were winning. The air was hot and thick and foul with cigarette smoke and intestinal gasses. Every few minutes a jet from the nearby airport would pass low overhead, rattling the thin walls. I was thinking about taking off myself, when someone knocked on the door.

Gibby let in an older guy, maybe thirty or thirty-five, with a deep suntan, short black hair, and a pink golf shirt covering a watermelon-size paunch. He wore a heavy-looking gold watch, and gold rings on most of his stubby fingers. His eyes were concealed behind a pair of wraparound sunglasses. A short, thick cigar jutted from his muscular lips.

Jason said, "Mr. Cigar! How are you doing?"

Later, I learned that the man's name was actually "Sicard." I don't know if Jason garbled the name or if I heard it wrong, but for the rest of the time he was there I thought of him as Mr. Cigar.

Cigar nodded at Jason. "Doin' good, kid." His voice was ragged, like he spent a lot of time yelling. Or maybe it was the cigars. He pointed at Jason's money. "That for me?"

Jason gave a nervous laugh. "I'll have it all for you pretty quick. I'm on a roll."

Nobody else was saying anything. In fact, it had gotten very quiet—not even the sound of Doughboy crunching Doritos.

"Hope you're right, kid." Cigar pulled up a chair and sat behind Jason. "Don't mind me, boys. Just keep playin'."

Doughboy shuffled the cards. "Five-card draw, deuces and fours wild," he announced.

Cigar laughed. It wasn't a nice laugh. He shook his head and muttered, "Deuces and fours wild." Like he couldn't believe anyone would actually play such a stupid game.

Doughboy stopped in midshuffle. "You want me to play something else?"

Cigar waved his cigar. "Don't mind me.

I'm just watchin.' You wanna deal wild-card games, that's your problem."

Doughboy looked down at the deck and said, "Five draw, nothing wild."

Jason said, "Hey, Dough, how about we up the stakes?"

Doughboy shrugged, sending a ripple up and down his body. "To what?"

"How about ten?"

"Okay with me."

"Me, too," said Gibby.

Sam looked unhappy about the higher stakes. He looked over at Cigar, took a breath, and said, "Okay. I guess."

I said it was okay with me, too, but I wasn't so sure. There were so many distractions—the heat, the airplanes, the cigar smoke, the noisy chatter—I couldn't concentrate. As I watched Doughboy deal the cards, I remembered something I had read:

> *The best poker players leave their emotions at home. They do not permit themselves to feel anger or fear or disappointment. They do not permit distractions to affect their play. The best players stand outside themselves.*

I looked at my cards. Three sevens.

I blocked out the tinny sound of Sam's Walkman and bet ten dollars.

Jason called. Cigar sat behind him, filling the air with blue smoke, a little smirk on his thick lips. I filtered out the smoke and the smirk and concentrated on Jason, reading him for a pair of tens, or possibly jacks. Gibby and Sam folded. Doughboy called. An airplane passing overhead shook the trailer, but I heard it only as a distant growl. Jason drew three, Doughboy drew one, and I drew two. I focused on Doughboy, looking for tells. Doughboy licked his lips, then wiped them with the back of a hand. I figured he hadn't got the card he wanted. Neither had I, but my three sevens still looked good. I bet again, they both called, and I won the pot, beating out Jason's tens and Doughboy's little two pair.

I watched my hands reach out and sweep in the money. Suddenly I was sure I was going to win. I was standing outside myself, my thoughts running clear and cold. I could have been in Doughboy's trailer, in Jason's bedroom, squatting in an alley, or sitting in a plush casino—it didn't matter. My universe began and ended at the card table.

We raised the stakes to twenty dollars, and I continued to win. Doughboy ran out of money and went into his mother's bedroom and came out with another fifty. Jason tapped out around nine-thirty and had to borrow a hundred from Cigar.

"You sure, kid?" asked Cigar. "I don't know if I like this. I come to collect the vig and here you're askin' for more."

"I'm good for it," Jason said.

Twenty minutes later he borrowed another hundred. And then another. Sam, after losing his last twenty-dollar bill, went outside and sat on the steps and cranked up his Walkman so loud we could hear it right through the screen door. Gibby stayed close to even for a while, then he began to lose, too.

Cigar stood up, shaking his head. "It's been real entertaining, kiddies, but I got to go." He pointed a thick index finger at Jason. "Do not disappoint me, kid."

"Don't worry," Jason said. "I'm good for it."

"That's what I tole the King."

After he left I asked, "Who was he?"

"He works for the King," Jason said. He stood up and started to open all the cabinets in the small kitchen.

Doughboy said, "Hey!"

Jason found what he was looking for

above the sink: a half-full bottle of vodka.

Doughboy said, "Hey, lay off that. That's my ma's."

Jason unscrewed the cap and took a gulp. He gasped and shook his head violently. "Whew! You got any orange juice to go with this?" His voice had gone hoarse.

"No! Put it back!"

"Don't worry about it. I'll get her a new bottle." Jason sat down and wedged the bottle between his legs. "We playing cards or what?"

Doughboy sighed and shuffled the deck. "She's gonna kill me," he muttered.

Gibby reached across the table. "Gimme a hit off that, Jase."

Jason passed the bottle.

"Who's the King?" I asked Jason.

"Mr. Kingston's the King."

"Oh." I had no idea who he was talking about. I asked, "What's a 'vig'?"

"You don't want to know," mumbled Jason. He grabbed the bottle back from Gibby and took another swallow.

The vodka did not make them better card players. My stack kept getting bigger. I busted Doughboy with a pair of kings. He opened a fresh bag of corn chips and glared at the three of us as we continued to play.

A few hands later I won the last of Jason's and Gibby's money on the same hand. They both had three-of-a-kind. I had a full house.

It was no contest.

Jason, watching me rake in the money, said, "Tell you what, Doylie, hows about we go double or nothing on everything you got." He threw an arm around my shoulder and breathed vodka and cigarettes in my face. "We flip a coin."

"No thanks," I said, shrugging off his arm. He kept talking, but I wasn't interested. Why should I take a fifty-fifty chance on losing? I finally said, "How about if we go home? Call it a night. I'm supposed to be home by midnight." I started stuffing the money into my pockets. I had more than nine hundred dollars.

Jason sneered. "You gonna turn into a pumpkin or something? It's only eleven-thirty."

I said, "Look, I don't want to play any-more. Besides, you don't have any money left."

"My IOU ain't good with you, Doylie?"

"I just don't feel like playing anymore," I said. I looked at Gibby. "Are you gonna give me a ride home?" Gibby hadn't had as much to drink as Jason. I figured he could still drive okay.

Gibby laced his hands behind his neck and leaned back in his chair. "I don't feel like driving," he said.

I stood there for a few seconds, not quite sure what to do. Jason was staring at me, his eyes red-rimmed and angry with loss and vodka. Gibby also had his eyes on me, but his face betrayed no emotion. Doughboy put a handful of corn chips into his fat face and crunched, his jaw moving slowly, grinding away like a Gila monster devouring a rat. Sam wouldn't look at me at all. A cold nugget of fear formed in my bowels. I looked at the door. Should I make a run for it? Then I felt ridiculous. These guys were my friends— maybe not good friends, but they weren't a bunch of thugs, either. If I ran for the door, they would laugh.

I said, "Well, I'm going home. I'll see you."

But my feet wouldn't move. I stood like a statue; the only sound was the soft, wet crunching coming from Doughboy's mouth.

Then Gibby laughed. It sounded like a dog barking. He said, "Go ahead, Doylie. Take your money and go."

I got the hell out of there.

To get home, I had to walk up Eastwood

Road to Airport Highway, then another mile over to Harrison.

Harrison Avenue is a narrow, winding road that connects the south end of the township, with its airport and trailer parks and industrial buildings, to the residential area where I lived. It doesn't get a lot of traffic at night. There are a few businesses near the airport end of the street—a tire company, an auto junkyard, and a pest control company—then the street dips down into a low-lying, marshy area with cottonwoods and cedars growing close against the side of the road and no lights and the air thick with mosquitoes and the roar of a million peeping frogs. The moon had not yet risen. The only light came from the stars.

I made my way along the shoulder as much by feel as by sight, asphalt under my left foot, the soft dirt shoulder under my right. I'd been walking about twenty minutes when a car approached from behind me. I stepped to the side to give it plenty of room. It blew past me going about eighty. Was it Gibby? The car was going so fast, I couldn't make it out. The taillights disappeared around the next bend, and the sound of the car faded. I continued my trek—asphalt, dirt, asphalt, dirt. After a few minutes I quit wondering about the car and started adding up my money.

One thousand dollars in the bank, plus two hundred I'd left in my bedroom, plus the nine hundred in my pocket added up to twenty-one hundred dollars. More money than I'd ever had in my life.

Another fifteen hundred and I'd be driving Harold Erickson's Camaro. I imagined myself behind the wheel. If I'd had that Camaro I'd have been home half an hour ago.

Fourteen hundred dollars. How hard could it be to come up with another fourteen hundred dollars? Another hundred-some hours of mowing lawns and trimming hedges would do it.

Or, better yet, a couple more good poker games.

I was fantasizing about that when a dark form appeared on the shoulder in front of me. I stopped, straining to see. I could make out the faint outline of a parked car. I heard a scuffing noise. I started to turn toward the sound when someone tackled me hard from behind. I went down, catching myself with one hand on the asphalt, the other hitting the dirt, and then I collapsed as his full weight came down on me, grinding my nose on the road. I think I shouted something before the sack went over my head and they started hitting me, fists or feet crashing into my ribs. I swung my fists, hitting nothing, then they got my arms behind my back and held them there and I felt more hands digging in my pockets.

They got it all.

A voice, distorted to sound like Donald Duck, told me to stay where I was and not move for ten minutes, "Or else!" I heard car doors opening and slamming shut. Just before the engine roared to life I heard a high-pitched, squawking laugh.

MR. HICKS

I told my mom that I'd fallen on my skateboard. I hadn't been on a skateboard since my encounter with Mr. Bus, but she didn't know that. Except for scrapes on my nose and hands, I didn't look too bad, but was I sore! After breakfast I went back to bed and lay awake for hours trying to figure out what to do, imagining all kinds of revenge. Every time I came up with an idea and thought how it might go, I ran into another dead end. The more I thought about it, the more it looked like I would never get a dime of that money back. A little before noon, I drifted off and didn't wake up until I felt a large weight sink onto the foot of my bed. I smelled peanuts and heard the sound of chewing. Without opening my eyes I said, "Hey, Murk."

"What the heck happened to you?" he asked. "And don't tell me you fell off your skateboard."

"I fell off my skateboard," I said.

"That's what your mom said. What happened really?"

I opened my eyes. Murky was eating some sort of peanut log about the size of a baseball bat.

I said, "I got beat up."

Murky's eyes widened. "By who?"

I told him everything. When I'd finished my story he was finished with his peanut log. He said, a hurt expression on his face, "You played poker and didn't invite me?"

I was surprised, but I shouldn't have been. Murky hated to be left out of anything, even if it was getting beat up and robbed.

"I didn't think you'd want to play," I said. "I mean, after last time. . . . "

"I had some bad luck."

"Uh, yeah, right. Anyways, it was a good thing you weren't there. Look what happened to me."

"If I was with you, they wouldn't have dared."

"Yeah, they'd have been real scared."

"So what are you gonna do?"

"I don't know."

"Well I know what *I'd* do. I'd go demand my money back."

"You think they're just going to give it to me?"

"You never know." Murky hopped off the bed. "You want me to go with you?"

A little while later, Murky and I were standing at Jason Hicks's front door.

"Press it again," he said.

"I don't think he's home."

"He's home." Murky reached past me and jabbed the doorbell five or six times. A few seconds later, the door opened.

Jason Hicks, even paler than usual, said, "What do you guys want?"

"I want my money back," I said.

Jason laughed. It was the exact same laugh I'd heard last night on Harrison Avenue. The sound of it made my heart start to pound even harder.

"What money?" he said. "You won all my money last night. I don't have any more."

"I know you're lying," I said. "I know it was you and your friends. If you don't give me the money, I'm going to the police."

Jason thought that was extra funny and he laughed so hard, he started to cough. When his coughing eased up, he said, "Doylie, I don't have any money, so you might as well forget it. Even if I did, I'd have to give it to the King. You're not the only one's got problems. You think you need money? You don't need it half as bad as me."

Right about then, Jason's father pulled into the driveway.

"You better get out of here," Jason said, suddenly looking worried. He started to close the door.

Murky, surprising me, said loudly, "We're not going anywhere until you give Denn his money back."

Mr. Hicks, who was just getting out of his car, asked, "What's going on here? What money?"

If Mr. Hicks had been a thing instead of a person, he would have been a bald tire with too much air in it. Even when he wasn't angry you could see the veins on his neck bulging and throbbing.

Jason said, "Nothin', Dad."

"You haven't been gambling again, I hope." Now we could see the veins popping out on his temples, too.

Jason shook his head.

Then Murky said, "He lost a lot of money to Denn here, Mr. Hicks, and last night him and his friends beat up Denn and stole his money. Nine hundred dollars."

Jason and I stared at Murky in disbelief. Of all the things I fantasized doing to get my money back, I'd never have considered spilling the beans to Mr. Hicks. It felt wrong. As for Mr. Hicks, he looked like he was going to blow for sure. New veins were popping out in places I didn't even know people *had* veins, like under his eyes and alongside his red nose.

He said, pointing a shaking finger at Murky, then at me, "You, you, get your sorry butts out of here. I don't ever want to see you near my son again." Before we could move he bulled past us, grabbed Jason by the arm, and slammed the door. Murky and I got our butts out of there. As we reached the sidewalk we heard the sharp sound of a slap and a yelp of pain.

I said, "What did you do *that* for?"

"What?"

"Tell Jason's dad. Now I'll never get a dime from him."

Murky shrugged. "You weren't gonna get anything anyway."

"Yeah, and now I'm probably going to get beat up again. I'll be looking over my shoulder the rest of my life."

TWENTIES

For the next couple days I acted like a jerk. When Murky called, I didn't call him back. When my mom asked me a question, I gave her a wiseass remark. I put off my lawn work at St. Luke's, and I told Mrs. Pratt I'd be a few days late mowing her lawn, and when the owner of the Claridge Apartments called and asked me if I'd like to do their gardening for one hundred dollars a month, I told them I didn't have the time. I talked to Kelly on the phone a couple times, but I just didn't have much to say. I spent a lot of time lying in bed reading poker books.

I told myself I was depressed because I'd lost nine hundred dollars.

But what really had me down was that I wouldn't be able to play any more poker with Jason and his friends.

The thought of going back to earning a few bucks an hour mowing lawns and trimming people's lilac bushes—my stomach turned at the thought.

Friday morning Seamus called and left a message saying that the grass was tickling his knees. I knew I couldn't put it off any longer. I called Murky and asked if he would help me get caught up with the gardening at St. Luke's.

"What's it pay?" he asked.

"I'll give you seven bucks an hour," I said. "That's seven bucks an hour more than I get."

Murky hemmed and hawed, then agreed to help.

With the two of us working, it went quickly. Murky wasn't as fast or neat as me, but we were done in two hours. Seamus came out with a cold pair of Cokes.

Murky drained his in one long swallow.

"Thanks," he belched.

Seamus grinned. "You must be Murky," he said. "I'm Father O'Gara. I appreciate your helping us out here."

"No problem," said Murk.

I said, "The trimming along the front walk is a little rough, but I'll clean it up next time." Murky had done that part of the trimming. He gave me a hurt look.

Seamus smiled sadly and shook his head. "It looks fine, Denn," he said. He turned back to Murky. "Alan Stein was your father, wasn't he?"

Murky nodded, a little startled.

"I knew Alan," said Seamus. "We worked together on a fund-raiser for a homeless shelter. That was a year before he passed on. He was a good man. He was very proud of you, I remember."

I thought Murky was going to start crying, but he didn't.

On the way home, I asked Murky if he wanted to help out with some of my other lawn jobs.

I could tell he was interested. He wanted to replace the bar mitzvah money he'd lost playing cards.

"You sure I won't be too sloppy for you?" he said.

"You'll get better."

The next morning after breakfast, my mom handed me an envelope. "Somebody put this in the mailbox," she said.

The envelope had my name and address scrawled on the front in pencil.

No return address.

Inside were three crisp twenty-dollar bills.

WATER

"So you don't know where it came from?" Kelly asked.

"No. At first I thought it was Fred, but the more I think about it, he wouldn't have mailed cash. He would've written a check so he could write it off his taxes. Also, he wouldn't hand-address an envelope. He'd have his secretary type it.

"It might be one of my customers prepaying me for some work. Like maybe they meant to put a note in the envelope, but forgot. I dunno. The only other thing I can think of is that maybe Jason got a guilty conscience."

"I don't think any of those boys *have* a conscience." Kelly stopped suddenly, picked up a twig, and coaxed a big green caterpillar off the dirt path.

"That thing'll probably grow up to be a big ugly moth," I said.

"At least it'll grow up to be something."

She watched until the thing crawled into the weeds. Kelly spent a lot of time worrying about the safety of bugs and things.

We were walking along the west bank of Beagle Creek. The temperature was in the nineties, but beneath the spreading cottonwoods with the icy waters of the creek rushing by, the air felt cool and comfortable. Kelly wore her Kennedy High School gym shorts and an ancient Grateful Dead T-shirt that she'd probably nabbed from her dad's dresser. She'd left her shoes back at the head of the path. Most of her hair was pulled back into a loose ponytail, but a few long wisps hung down along her cheek, sticking a little to the sheen of perspiration. Every now and then she would reach up and tuck the stray hairs up over her ear, but they wouldn't stay.

"What are you going to do with the money?" she asked.

"Put it in the bank, I suppose. Sooner or later I'll find out who sent it to me."

"As long as you don't play poker with it."

That hit me wrong. It bugged me that she would rub it in that way, and that she would tell me what I could do with my money.

"Maybe I'll go out to the Indian casino and put it all in the slot machines," I said.

"Ha-ha." Kelly stepped off the path, over a

big gray rock, and into the creek. "Wow, you should try this. It feels good."

"No thanks," I said. "I don't want to lose any toes to those snapping turtles."

Kelly let out a squeak and jumped up on the rock. I laughed.

She pushed out her lower lip. "There aren't any snapping turtles in there."

I laughed. "Oh yes there are. Snappers and giant water bugs and cottonmouth snakes, too."

She stepped back onto the path, and we continued our walk. All the little sticks and bits of leaves and grains of dirt stuck to Kelly's wet feet.

She said, "You wouldn't really go play slot machines, would you?"

"Nah. I don't think the odds are any good. I think if I was gonna go to the casino, I'd probably just play poker."

Kelly gave me a swat on the arm, then tried to push me into the creek. I grabbed her and we swung around, laughing, trying to dump each other in the chilly water—but not trying too hard. Then my foot hit a slippery spot on a rock and I went flailing backward, and Kelly lost her balance too, and we both fell full-length into the creek.

The water was sharp and cold as an electric shock.

It felt great.

I stopped by St. Luke's later that afternoon. Murky had done a slapdash job on the bushes near the front entrance, and I thought Seamus would appreciate a little touch-up before Sunday services. He heard my clippers and came out onto the front steps wearing his black priest robe and holding a plastic pitcher, the kind used for watering houseplants.

"How's it going, Denn?"

I told him it was going great, except that his bushes needed some trimming.

Seamus regarded the bushes. "I thought your friend did a passable job. You know, Denn, they don't have to be perfect."

"It'll just take me a couple minutes."

Seamus sat down on the steps. "Uh-huh. I hear you've been playing some cards lately."

"Where'd you hear that?"

"I was talking to Sam Grant's father. He's on the church board. He said you and some of Sam's friends have been gambling up a storm."

"Oh."

"I used to play some poker, back in seminary."

"Did you win much?"

"Sometimes I won, sometimes I lost. After a while it just didn't matter. If I lost I felt stupid.

If I won I felt bad for the guys who lost. It was sort of a lose-lose situation."

"I feel good when I win."

"Then I hope you win all the time."

"Me, too." I looked at the pitcher in his hands. "Watering the plants?"

"In a sense. I was filling up the holy water receptacles."

"That's *holy* water?"

Seamus stood up and raised the pitcher. "Very holy. A few drops of this in the right place, no more sin." He grinned and winked.

That night I picked up the ringing phone, thinking it would be Murky or Kelly, but it was Fred.

"Hey, sport! You never called me back!"

"Uh, sorry, Fred. I got busy."

"I know how that goes. Sometimes I look at my watch, I don't know if it's A.M. or P.M. How's your mom?"

"She's okay."

"And you? What are you busy with? Can't be school, it's, cripes, is it almost July? I guess it is, it got up to a hundred degrees out here today. Lawn business? That what you're busy with?"

"Yeah. Really busy. So what did you call about?"

"I was wondering whether you'd like to come out and see me. I got a place on the beach here. You could learn to surf, or we could visit a couple movie sets. You know. Spend a little time with the old man." He laughed.

Not all tells are visual. When a poker player raises his voice a little too loud, it tells you he's nervous. Sometimes it means he's bluffing, and sometimes it means he's afraid for some other reason. But the louder a guy talks, the scareder he is, and Fred was practically bruising my eardrum.

"Just for a couple weeks, sport," he said.

"I'm kinda busy—"

"I know, I know. Can't you get that buddy of yours to help you out? Marky?"

"It's Murky. And I don't think so." I tried to change the subject. "Hey, Fred? What's a 'vig'?"

"Vig? That's what loan sharks call the interest on a loan. Why?"

"I heard it in a movie."

"Oh. Well, how about you come out for just a week, then. I'd like to see you, Denn."

"Why don't you come here?"

That shut him up for a few seconds. We both knew why he didn't want to come back to Fairview. It was because my mom would be all over him trying to get him back.

"Look, sport, I know you're mad at me."

"I'm not mad."

"You think I just abandoned you and your mom. Maybe in a way I did, but you have to understand something, champ—I spent fifteen years working for that ad agency in Fairview, writing copy for cereal boxes when what I wanted to do was come out here and write scripts for movies. When I finally got my shot, I had to take it. It's what I'm good at, champ. And I'm damn good. I just sold a script for two hundred thousand dollars. How many guys get a chance to chase their dreams and make that kind of money?"

"You could have brought us with you."

"This is no place to raise a family, champ. Your mom wouldn't have been happy here. Besides, I needed to get away. I know you don't understand, but when you get older, you will."

Of all the things adults say to kids, that has got to be the all-time stupidest.

I said, "Maybe when I'm dead I'll understand everything."

"Don't talk like that. Denn, I know I haven't been a great father to you, but I'm trying. Why don't you take a couple days off, hop on a plane. I'll send you a ticket." He paused. "There's someone I want you to meet."

"Who? If it's Arnold Schwarzenegger, I'll come."

"Her name is Cindy."

"Oh." That gave me a weird feeling just above my stomach. "I'm really too busy, Fred. Maybe we could do it next year."

He tried to argue with me, but I told him the bathtub was overflowing and I hung up. I went upstairs. The tub was bone-dry. I took off all my clothes and got in the shower and turned on the water as hot as I could stand it. I sat on the tile floor and let the hot water rain down on me, thinking about Fred. I imagined myself playing poker with him, taking all his money, reading his facial expressions the way I'd been able to read Jason and Doughboy and Gibby and Sam. I thought about Mr. Cigar wanting to "collect the vig" from Jason. I wondered when I would have a chance to play cards again, and who I would be playing against. I sat on the floor of that shower until it ran as cold as the waters of Beagle Creek.

SAM

One week later I saw Sam Grant sitting by himself at the Burger King, rocking out with his Walkman, eating french fries. I brought my tray over to his table and sat down.

Sam did not look happy to see me. I sucked down half my Pepsi and waited for him to turn down his Walkman. After a few seconds, he did.

"How's it going?" Sam asked.

"Pretty good."

We sat there for a long time without either of us saying anything, then Sam blurted out, "Look, Denn, I didn't have no part of what happened to you. I was in the back of the car the whole time. I didn't know what they were gonna do. I mean, Jason was loaded, and Gibby was pretty messed up, too. I was just hoping he wouldn't drive the car into the swamp or something, you know? When we stopped I thought they were just gonna scare you. I just sat in the car."

"Yeah, right," I said. But I half believed him. I figured Sam for an okay guy, not mean-hearted and dangerous like Gibby, or desperate like Jason. He was just a guy.

"Anyways, I'm real sorry."

"You sorry enough to give me my money back?"

"I didn't take any. Gibby and Jase split it up, then we drove out to Marcel's and Jason gave his half to Mr. Sicard.

"Sicard? The cigar guy?"

"Yeah, the guy that works for Mr. Kingston."

"Who is this Kingston, anyway?"

"He runs the poker game at Marcel's. Jason lost a bunch of money to him last month."

I'd thought it might be something like that. "So when's the next game?"

Sam looked startled. "You—you want to play?" Like he couldn't believe it.

"Not really," I lied.

"That's what I figured. Me either. You know your friend Murky?"

"Yeah?"

"He played over at Gibby's last night. Lost about five hundred bucks. There's a guy shouldn't gamble, man. You oughta talk to him. He don't know how to quit."

I was stunned. Murky had lost five hundred dollars? He must be suicidal.

"I will," I said. I took a big bite out of my Whopper.

Sam stood up. "Later, dude," he said.

I swallowed and said, "Just a sec, Sam. I was wondering if you could do me a favor."

He frowned. "What?"

I licked my lips. Now *I* was nervous. I said, "You know where I can get a fake ID?"

Watching Murky mow a lawn was like watching a goat give a haircut. The only good thing you could say was that there was less grass when he was done than there'd been when he'd started.

"Take your time, Murk. Try to push the mower in a straight line."

"That's what I'm *doing*!" he shouted over the roar of the mower.

I shook my head and returned to trimming Mrs. Pratt's front walk. There would be no ten-dollar tip for this job. Not unless the old lady had lost her glasses again. Sooner or later, Murky would get the hang of it. It wasn't my concern. I was giving him my customers one by one. He'd either make it or he wouldn't.

One thing I have to say—he was working hard. Losing a chunk of his bar mitzvah money had hit Murky hard. He felt sick about the money, and he was terrified that his mother would find out.

Fortunately for Murky, it was Denn Doyle to the rescue. If he learned the business and worked hard, by the time school started he could make up all the money he'd lost, and then some.

As for me, I was sick of cutting grass.

I had other plans.

PART TWO
JULY

SWANEE

Cookie raised ten.

Dragon Lady called.

So did Tic-Tac, Smitty, K. C., and the guy from New York.

I raised another ten dollars and got calls all around. Chuckie, the dealer, tapped the deck and flopped three: jack, ten, deuce. Two of the cards were spades. I wasn't worried about Dragon Lady, Smitty, or Tic-Tac, but I watched Cookie, K. C., and the guy from New York. Cookie was a tough player. I didn't know the guy from New York. This was the first time I'd seen him at The Magic Hand.

The corners of Cookie's mouth pulled in about a hundredth of an inch. Could be he liked his cards. With Cookie, it was hard to tell.

The guy from New York picked up two ten-dollar chips, even though he would be the last bettor. We were all supposed to notice that. He wanted us to think he was going to raise, but what it really meant was that his hand was just so-so, and he was trying to scare us off our bets.

Kid stuff. The guy from New York didn't worry me so much anymore.

"Your bet, Swanee," the dealer said to me.

We were playing hold 'em, a poker game where each player gets two cards facedown. Three more "up-cards" are then turned faceup on the table. That's called "the flop." All the players use those up-cards to make their hands. Then a fourth and fifth card are dealt face-up, with bets after each. The player who can come up with the best five-card hand wins.

I bet. With a jack, ten in my hand plus the jack, ten on the table, I was the odds-on favorite to win.

Dragon Lady folded, tossing her cards to Chuckie with a jangle of her gold bracelets. "My pair no good," she said. "Cards bad. I have bad luck all week." I smiled at Dragon Lady's act. She was one of the sharpest poker players at the Hand.

Cookie, who I figured to have an ace, king, took a close look at me, grunted, and threw his cards away. K. C., Tic-Tac, and New York all called.

The fourth card came up the eight of hearts. I bet twenty.

Smitty and New York called. K. C. and Tic-Tac folded. They'd probably been hoping for another spade. The last card was another ten, giving me a full house. Smitty and the guy from New York called my bet, but they didn't look too happy about it. Smitty had three tens. I showed my full boat. New York slapped his hand down with a curse—he had a straight. Chuckie pushed a nice little pot in my direction. I tipped him a one-dollar chip. He rapped the chip on the edge of the table and dropped it into his sagging shirt pocket. "Thanks, Swanee."

I stacked my chips. So far that night I was up $250.

It beat the hell out of mowing lawns.

It was Cookie gave me the name Swanee.

The first time I visited the Hand, I'd dressed up in an old herringbone sport coat, a white dress shirt, and a blue silk tie covered with wavy white shapes. Fred had taken most of his clothes when he'd left, but there were still a few things hanging in his closet. I was pretending to be an adult, so I figured I'd better dress like one. I was so scared, I practically wet my pants when the guard at the door inspected my fake ID, then gave me this long, suspicious look. I looked right back at him and pretended I was bluffing with a pair of deuces. It must've worked, 'cause I got in.

It turned out I was the only customer in the whole casino wearing a tie.

A few minutes later I was sitting at a long green table playing seven-card stud. To my left sat a man so old and pale and unhealthy looking, I was afraid he would die right there at the table. An unlit cigar about ten inches long hung from his slack lips, and I could hear his every wheezing breath. He smelled of peppermint.

The first few hands I was so nervous, my hands were shaking. I just folded every time the bet came to me. Then I got dealt a pair of kings and the woman to my right bet ten and I heard myself saying, "Raise ten."

The old guy looked at his cards, then at mine. He frowned, then spoke around his cigar. "What do you got under dere, Swanee?"

"I don't know," I said. My hands had steadied. I was glad he couldn't see my shaking knees. "I forgot."

"Yeah, I bet you did. I call you anyways, Swanee."

I don't remember how the rest of that hand went, but I won, and for the rest of the night everybody called me "Swanee." When I got home and took off that stupid tie I saw that the design on it, if you looked real close, was a bunch of flying swans. I knew then why the old guy, who I later learned was called Cookie, had given me my nickname.

I also knew why Fred had left the tie behind.

In time, the guards at the front door of The Magic Hand came to know me. They never asked to see my fake ID anymore, and I put away the sport coat and tie. As long as I filled a seat at the poker table and behaved myself and tipped the dealers now and then, they didn't much care who I was or what I looked like.

I was a regular.

Playing in a casino, I soon learned, is a lot different than playing in somebody's kitchen. Casino poker is fast—a new hand gets dealt every two minutes. The average casino player is a lot older, smarter, and more patient than the high school kids I was used to playing with. They don't give a lot away. But once you peel back those layers of years and experience you find nothing but a bunch of kids playing a grown-up game. Their tells are more subtle and deceptive, but if you know what to look for, you'll find them.

I did. I'd been playing five nights a week, and winning.

I heard the dealer say, "Ten dollars to you, Swanee."

I'd been dealt a new hand. I peeked at my cards.

"Raise it up," I said, tossing a green chip toward the pot.

GOLDEN

The cab dropped me off at my house about midnight. All the lights were out. That was good. I let myself in and closed the door quietly. After the smoke and noise of The Magic Hand, the house seemed eerily quiet and clean. I stood in the living room, breathing the familiar air.

"Denn?" my mother's quavery voice floated in from the kitchen.

I sighed and said, "It's me."

She was in her usual chair, in her bathrobe, holding an empty teacup. I poured myself a glass of juice and sat down across from her.

"How was work?" she asked.

"Okay," I said.

She smiled. "I wish you didn't have to work so late, honey. I worry about you."

I shrugged. We'd had this conversation so many times, I was sick of it.

"Way out there at that casino," she continued, "all those people gambling. I'm not so sure I like that, Denn."

"Mom, we've talked about this. The people there are nice. Besides, all I do is sweep up and empty ashtrays and stuff." Lying didn't come naturally to me, but it was getting easier.

"It just doesn't seem like a good place for a boy your age. And I don't like how they make you stay so late some nights."

I yawned. "Can we talk about this later? I'm really beat." I put my juice glass in the sink.

"I spoke with your father about this, Denn, and he agrees with me."

That stopped me.

"You talked to Fred?"

She nodded. "He told me you haven't been returning his calls. I want you to talk to him tomorrow, Denn."

"Fine," I said. "I'll talk to him." I went to my room and sat on my bed and stared at the wall until my eyes hurt. Then I pulled the night's winnings out of my pocket and counted.

Six hundred forty dollars.

Except for my mom getting on my case, it had been a great night. My best night since that time at Doughboy's. In one way, it was even better.

At The Magic Hand, they let you keep the money.

I slept in the next morning. When I finally woke up I just lay there for about an hour. Why bother to get up? I'd given Murky my lawn business, so I didn't have to go hack at foliage. I could hear my mom knocking around the house, cleaning. I was in no great hurry to continue last night's conversation, so I just fantasized about betting thousands of dollars, playing with the pros.

Sometime around noon I heard the car start and back out of the driveway. She was probably going shopping. I got up and made myself a pancake. While it was cooking, I checked the mailbox. Some bills and stuff for my mom, and one familiar-looking envelope with my name on it. I tore it open. Three twenties, just like every Friday for the past four weeks.

I stuffed the twenties in my pocket and went back to check on my pancake.

The phone rang. I answered, hoping it wasn't Fred. "Hello?"

"Hi!"

It was Kelly.

"Hi yourself. What's going on?" I lifted the edge of the pancake. Too soon to flip it.

"Nothing much."

"I won again last night," I said.

"Playing poker?"

"Yeah. I actually got a straight flush one hand. That's only happened to me once before."

"That's great, Denn." She sounded bored.

I'd noticed that before. When I tried to talk to her about cards Kelly quickly lost interest. It was like when she tried to talk to me about the kids she was working with at the wheelchair camp on Lake Winonah. I just didn't care about a bunch of little kids, in or out of wheelchairs. But I knew she would want to tell me all about her job, so I said, "How are things at the camp? Any of the kids roll off the dock in their wheelchairs?"

"That's not funny, Denn."

I flipped the pancake. "Perfect!"

"What?"

"My pancake is perfect."

"Oh."

"Hey—what's the date today?"

"The fifteenth."

"Tomorrow's your birthday! I'm taking you out to dinner, right?"

"Are you sure you still want to?"

"Sure I'm sure. Why wouldn't I be?" The truth was, I hadn't thought about Kelly's "golden birthday" since I'd promised to take her to Marcel's, and that was a month ago. If she hadn't called I would have spaced it completely.

"I haven't heard much from you lately, Denn. I thought maybe you, you know. I mean, I don't know."

"I've been busy."

"I called you two days ago and you never called me back."

"I didn't?" I remembered her message on the answering machine. Hadn't I called her back? I thought I had. "I must not have got your message."

Kelly didn't say anything for a few seconds, but I could hear her breathing.

I said, "Well? Are we on?"

"I guess. If you want. But I'm still mad at you."

"Oh. Uh, how about I pick you up at twenty to eight?"

"What should I wear?"

"It's your b-day, you can wear what you want. I'm gonna put on a sport coat. But I'm not wearing a tie." I'd learned my lesson, tie-wise. "I gotta go. My pancake is ready."

We hung up, and I flopped the cake out onto a plate and globbed a quarter stick of butter on top. I sat and watched it melt, thinking about how hard it was to keep people happy. I watched the butter melt until it became a puddle of greasy gold.

The two saleswomen at Bjork Jewelers went into action as soon as I walked in the door. I saw them exchange glances, then take up defensive positions—the older one with the big orange hair stood near the cash register pretending to read receipts, and the blond one moved to the end of the display case. I walked slowly down the glass display, letting my eyes take in their glittering contents—silver and red and gold and green—the prices were written on tiny paper tags. It made me think of scattered playing cards, all colors and numbers and money. I stopped in front of an array of gold jewelry and waited for one of them to acknowledge that I was a human being.

The younger one finally spoke.

"Can I help you?" The tone of her voice implied that she didn't think she could.

I pointed. "May I see that?"

"The—the necklace?" I saw her look at the orange-haired woman, who frowned, then nodded. The blond woman unlocked the case. She brought out a velvet tray and placed it atop the glass case. I stared at it for a moment, then slipped my fingers into the loop of gold chains and raised it slowly from the blue velvet. A cascade of pure gold droplets caught the fluorescent light, giving off a soft rattle, shimmering like hot metal rain.

The saleswoman forgot for a moment that I was a dangerous, wild-eyed teenager and smiled. "The piece was designed by Leroy LaFortunato," she said. "He calls it 'the Golden Fall.' Each of the five chains has eighteen beads, ninety in all, to represent the days of autumn."

"It looks like rain," I said.

"It's a very beautiful piece." Her face hardened as she remembered who she was dealing with. "It's rather expensive," she added. "Each bead is hand-thrown in pure twenty-four-carat gold."

I pulled the roll of hundred-dollar bills from my jeans. Pure gold. The perfect gift for a golden birthday. Kelly would be so knocked out, she'd forget all about being mad at me. Dealing with people, I thought, was a lot like playing cards. Sometimes you'd lose, but then you get dealt a few good cards and you're golden.

AGENDA

On the way home I walked past St. Luke's. The grass was cut, the edges were trimmed, and there was new mulch around the rose-bushes, but things looked a little rough—you could tell that Denn Doyle wasn't in charge anymore. It was a Murk job if ever I saw one.

Part of me felt embarrassed. Another part of me liked the fact that Murky couldn't make things look as good as I could. I walked back to the cemetery and sat on the stone wall and looked at all the ragged clumps of grass he'd missed.

I hadn't seen Murk in two weeks. The last time we'd talked, I'd been telling him about how much money I was winning at the Hand, and he'd just made some remark about how he had to "earn" his money. Like playing good cards wasn't hard work. Our lives had come to a fork in the road. I was following the superhighway, and Murky was stumbling down a cow path. I felt sorry for him, mowing all those lawns, chasing the bar mitzvah money he'd lost because he was a lousy card player.

I'd been sitting there a while when I looked up and saw a man in running shorts and a Nike T-shirt jogging past. He saw me and stopped. It took me a second to get past the long, hairy legs and the headband to recognize Seamus.

"Hey, Denn!" He walked over, soaked with sweat. "Haven't seen you in a while." He propped his sweaty butt on Frances Maccabee's tombstone.

"You training or something?" I asked.

"Actually, yes. I'm going to run the New York City Marathon this November. I've been logging about sixty miles a week."

"That sounds like a tough way to get to no place."

"True!" He laughed. "Keeps me out of trouble, though. How have you been? Keeping busy?"

"Yeah. I see Murky's been keeping your grass down."

"He's a good kid."

I couldn't help saying, "Kinda sloppy, though."

Seamus raised his black eyebrows. "Oh? It

looks good to me. He's going gangbusters with the lawn business."

"Really?" That didn't sound like the Murky I knew.

"He has a partner now. You know Tyler Kitterage, don't you?"

I nodded. I hadn't seen Ty since those first poker games at Jason's.

"Ty and Mark are mowing half the lawns on the north side. They bought a riding mower and they're using Ty's old pickup truck. Mark told me they're clearing eight hundred dollars a week. Sometimes I think that boy likes money more than you do, Denn."

"Is he still taking care of you for free?"

Seamus laughed. "Nothing is for free, Denn. What have you been up to lately?"

I had the urge to pull the necklace out of my pocket to show him. I wanted to tell him that I was making so much money, I could buy my girlfriend a sixteen-hundred-dollar necklace. I wanted Seamus to know that I was doing better than Murky. But I figured that I'd just get some kind of lecture, so I kept the gold in my pocket.

"Nothing much. I got a job out at the casino."

"Oh? I didn't think they hired anyone under eighteen."

"Well, they do." I stood up. "I gotta go."

I felt lousy after talking to Seamus and I didn't know why. Maybe it was the fact that Murky had made a success out of my little lawn business. But why should that bug me? He was working his butt off for eight hundred a week, which he then had to split with Ty Kitterage. I could make that in a few hours at the card table.

Since last month my financial situation had improved radically. Four weeks ago I'd had a total of twelve hundred dollars to my name. Now, after a few weeks at The Magic Hand, I had four grand in the bank, plus another thousand in cash, and that was after paying for Kelly's necklace. I was winning money practically every night, plus I was finding sixty dollars in cash every week in the mailbox. Why should I begrudge Murky his paltry few dollars?

But I did. Murky's cow path was getting wider, and I resented it.

I should have been happy for him, but I wasn't.

The thing is, when you're playing poker, you want to win. I guess I wanted to win more than anything.

* * *

When I got home my mom was talking on the phone. As soon as I walked in the kitchen, she handed it to me.

I said, "Hello?"

"Hey there, sport!"

"Hi, Fred."

"You think about what we talked about? About you coming out here for a visit?"

"Uh, I don't think I can." I wandered into the living room and sank into the sofa.

"Why not? Your mom tells me you sold your lawn business to your friend Mark."

"I sort of gave it to him. I got a job now."

"That's what I hear."

"Yeah." I didn't want to get into it, so I changed the subject. "Can I ask you something?"

"Anything, sport."

"You used to take Mom to Marcel's sometimes, didn't you?"

"Whenever I was feeling rich!" He laughed. "Why?"

"I'm taking Kelly out for her birthday. Do I have to wear a tie?"

"A tie? I wouldn't think so." He laughed again. "You're taking her to Marcel's? That's a pretty nice birthday present. Of course, since you won't be drinking any wine you should be able to get out of there for under a hundred bucks."

"I bought her a necklace, too."

"Hey, big spender!"

"So, what should I order?"

"Order?"

"From the menu. Like, what kind of food do they have?"

"At Marcel's? Continental, mostly. A lot of beef and veal dishes. They're known for their"—it sounded like he said—"steak a pwahv."

"What's that?"

"Pepper steak. But everything's quite good if you like the heavier French cuisine."

"Oh, yeah, I love the heavier French cuisine." Especially french fries and Le Big Mac, I thought.

"If you see Marcel, say hello for me."

"You know him?"

"Marcel Kaporsky? Sure. Actually, I'm surprised he's still in business. He was having some financial problems a few years back. He's a great cook, but he has a little gambling problem. You've probably seen him around that casino."

"Maybe. I wouldn't know what he looks like."

"He's a little guy with a mustache, always looks like he just ate a lemon."

That sounded like a lot of guys I'd seen

around the casino. "I'll look for him," I said.

"He used to run a poker game in one of the private rooms at his restaurant. Big money. I doubt he's still doing it, since every time he played he lost. I could never figure out why a smart guy like Marcel would want to play cards with some of those lowlifes. One of my clients got into one of those games once and nearly lost his house. Anyway, my guess is that Marcel has cleaned up his act, or they'd be calling the restaurant Kingston's by now."

I felt as if I'd swallowed a big lump of ice. "Kingston's?"

"One of the guys who used to play cards with Marcel. A professional gambler. Look, I don't want to bore you with a bunch of ancient history. I'm sure the food's still top-notch. You have a good time with Kelly."

"Thanks."

"You sure you won't come out for a visit?"

I came back to reality and landed hard. All the warm feelings I'd been having went out of me with a whoosh. This was Fred I was talking to. You couldn't just talk to him. Fred *always* had an agenda.

I said, "I don't know. I think I'd rather stay here. I'm pretty busy."

"Just for a weekend, then. I'll send you a ticket. Whaddyasay, sport?"

"Um, I guess . . ."

"Good! Next weekend, then?"

"You mean tomorrow?"

"No, no, you've got a date with your girl then! I mean the one after that."

"Uh, how about the one after *that*?"

"Fine! Fine! I'm really looking forward to this, champ. You're gonna love LA."

When I hung up the phone my mother was looking at me with a peculiar expression on her face.

"You know," she said, "you look more like your father every day."

SNAILS

They seated us at a table near the kitchen where every thirty seconds this door banged open and a waiter came charging past us with a tray the size of a card table. I didn't like that much, but Kelly thought it was funny.

"They're so *serious*," she said.

She was right. Everybody at Marcel's was serious. Old and serious. The menus were serious, too—about two feet tall and bound in red leather. Or maybe it was vinyl.

"It's really *expensive*," Kelly said. "What's *tournedos de boeuf*?"

"Some kind of meat, I think. Should we get an appetizer?"

"I don't know what any of these things are."

"How about the *escargot*?"

"Isn't that snails?"

"Yeah. I've never eaten a snail. Should we do it?"

"You can. I think I'm going to have a

salad." She shivered and rubbed her upper arms. "It's cold in here."

I looked up at the source of the cool air. We were sitting beneath an air-conditioning vent. Kelly was wearing a green dress with thin straps over her freckled shoulders.

Our very serious and polite waiter appeared. Kelly ordered a *salade verte* and I asked for the *escargot*.

"Very good, sir," said the waiter.

"And could you turn the AC down a little? We're cold."

"Of course, sir."

"And we'd like a bottle of wine," I added. Kelly's eyes widened.

The waiter said, "We have a very nice Catawba, sir."

"That will be fine. Is Marcel here this evening?"

"I'm sorry, sir, but Monsieur Marcel is no longer with Marcel's." Offering no further explanation, the waiter turned and left.

"You ordered *wine*?" Kelly said.

"I figured it was worth a shot." I wondered where the private dining rooms were located. Now that Marcel was "no longer with Marcel's," did the poker game still go on?

"Well, it sounds like he's going to bring us some." She hugged herself, shivering.

"I think Catawba is more like fizzy grape juice." I pushed my chair back. "I have to visit the rest room. Back in a minute."

The men's room was enormous—three brass sinks, stalls with wooden doors, and urinals filled with crystal-clear ice cubes. A uniformed attendant stood beside a pile of fluffy white towels. I used one of the urinals, then washed my hands. As I did so, the attendant draped a towel over my shoulder.

"Thank you," I said. Then I recognized Jason Hicks, and my mouth fell open. I took in his uniform: maroon jacket with gold braid, navy pants with light blue piping. "This is what you do here?"

"That's right," Jason said. He flicked imaginary lint from the shoulders of my sport coat with a soft brush. "You must be doing okay, Doylie. I hear you been killin' 'em at the Hand." He gave me a look of weary resentment, the way he might look at someone else's winning poker hand after losing a big pot.

"It's a lot safer playing at the casino," I said. "They don't beat me up and steal my money when I win."

Jason's cheek twitched; he licked his lips. "Everybody's got money troubles, man. I'm workin' two jobs and getting nowhere."

I had a feeling it was Jason who was dropping sixty dollars in my mailbox every week. I said, "Anyways, I appreciate the sixty bucks every week."

Jason flushed. "What sixty?"

If we'd been playing cards, I'd have called his bluff, but I just said, "Nothing. Never mind." If he didn't want me to know it was him leaving the money, that was his business. I went for the door, then stopped. "Hey, Jason. Do they still have that big poker game here?"

A shadow passed across his face. "What about it?"

"I was just curious. Where do they play?"

"Around back. Private entrance. They play Friday and Saturday. Invitation only."

The door opened, and a flustered man came in and showed Jason a spot of sauce on his shirt cuff. Jason went to work on the stain; I returned to the dining room.

Kelly was still studying the menu.

"See anything you like?"

Kelly frowned. "Everything is so expensive."

"Don't worry about the money, Kell."

"Well, I think you should let me pay for half."

"No way! This is your golden birthday." I took the gift-wrapped box out of my pocket and placed it in front of her.

"A present?" She looked at it, picked it up, set it down.

"Open it."

She removed the wrapping paper slowly, folding it neatly before opening the gray velvet box.

I don't know what I expected. Maybe I thought she was going to leap across the table and hug me. Or start crying tears of joy. Or jump into the air and scream in happiness. It was such a perfect gift. But what Kelly did was stare at it for almost a minute, saying nothing.

I said, "For your golden birthday."

"It's gold?"

"Pure gold."

She nodded, then closed the box. "I can't accept this, Denn. It's just too much."

I got a huge hollow feeling inside.

Just then the waiter appeared with our bottle of Catawba. He uncorked it and poured a little into my wineglass for me to sample. It tasted like grape soda. "An excellent year," I said. Kelly laughed politely. The waiter filled our glasses, then asked if we had selected our entrées.

"Do you have, like, chicken breast?" Kelly asked.

"Indeed we do," said the waiter. He went

on to describe something called *poulet chaud-froid*. It sounded awful—cold chicken in some sort of white sauce—but Kelly went ahead and ordered it. I asked for the *steak au poivre*, trying to remember how Fred had pronounced it. It came out sounding like "steak-approve," but he seemed to know what I meant.

When I looked back at Kelly, she was staring at me like I had a bug on my face.

"Denn . . . I'm serious about this. I mean, I really appreciate it, but it would feel too weird, wearing something like this. It must've cost you hundreds of dollars."

Hundreds? I started talking then, telling her how much I wanted her to have the necklace, how good it would look on her, how she would only have one golden birthday her entire life. Somewhere in my babbling I told her how much the necklace had really cost. Then I tried to cover that up by telling her the cost wasn't important because of how much money I'd been making and that the money was nothing to me, just green paper, and that I wanted her to have this necklace and not to worry about the money because I had a lot of it and I could get more.

Kelly said, "Denn, I know you've won a lot of money at that casino. But it's changing you. I mean, you've always liked money, but you're, like, obsessed with it now. You're turning into this other person."

"You don't get it," I told her. "What I'm trying to explain to you is that the money is nothing but a way to keep score. I've got a *talent* for poker. I've never been this good at anything before. I'm the best, Kell. Some of these guys, they've been playing for fifty years, and I can still beat them any day of the week. I'm thinking about not going back to school this fall."

Kelly's eyes widened. "Are you serious?"

"Maybe I am. I've never been this good at anything before, Kell. When I'm playing cards it's like . . . it's like I'm where I'm supposed to be."

Kelly blinked. I could see she didn't get it. "Well, that's fine," she said. "Only I don't think you should drop out of school, and you can't just ignore everybody all the time. I don't hear from you for days at a time, and when I try to talk about my work—what I do is important to me, Denn—you tune me out."

"No, I don't. I hear everything you say."

"Yeah, but you don't *care.* And look how you've treated poor Murky, your best friend."

"What are you talking about? I gave him my lawn business to help him out, didn't I?"

"You threw it to him like an old shirt you didn't want to wear anymore, Denn."

I could see I was losing her and I started babbling, telling her the whole reason I wanted money was so I could buy a car so we could go out on real dates. Go for drives along the river. And I wasn't talking about Harold Erickson's old Camaro—I already had enough money for that, but with all the money coming my way I'd decided to go for a brand-new Camaro with a T-top and a six-speed. With every word I said, her eyes grew more distant. I was watching the words run out of my mouth, building a wall between us. I couldn't stop myself. Everything I said made me sound stupider. Then the waiter's hand appeared, and a cloud of steaming garlic hit me in the back of my throat. I clamped my mouth shut and stared down at a plate containing six enormous snails swimming in hot molten butter.

"L'escargot," said the waiter.

CRAWL

I ate three of them. I ate the first one because I didn't know what else to do. I ate the second one to show off, and the third because they'd cost twelve dollars and fifty cents. Kelly picked at her salad and watched the snails crawl down my throat. After the third one she stood up and said she had to go to the ladies' room.

She was gone a long time. I drank half of the Catawba, but I left the remaining snails alone. Waiters whooshed past me, carrying strange-looking meals to the other tables.

A tall, narrow-featured man wearing a dark suit glided from table to table, greeting people. When he smiled his mouth changed shape, but the rest of his face remained immobile, as if frozen or carved from stone. I watched him, wondering if he would stop at our table. Maybe I would ask him what had happened to Marcel. But before he got to me, his attention was captured by a man standing at the other side off the dining room near the front door.

It was Sicard—Mr. Cigar—wearing a yellow golf shirt under a bright green sport coat. Sicard and the stone-faced man spoke for a moment, then a waiter led Sicard to a table near the wall, just ten feet away from me. Our eyes touched, but he didn't seem to recognize me.

I poured myself more Catawba. The waiter came by, whisking away my unfinished *escargot*. A blast of cold air from the air-conditioning vent hit my neck and sent a chill down my body. The waiter had never turned it down.

I suddenly felt like a little kid—small and alone. What was I doing sitting here in this fancy restaurant? I wished that I'd taken Kelly to a movie or something, where we could eat popcorn and laugh and maybe go out for pizza afterward, or go for a walk along the banks of Beagle Creek. I wished I'd bought her a pair of earrings, something fun and inexpensive. I wished we were dressed in jeans and T-shirts instead of me in this stupid sport coat and Kelly cold in her little green dress. I wished I was still mowing lawns and hanging out with Murky at the mall, just goofing around and acting like a couple of idiots and having fun.

But I wasn't. Somehow I had landed in

this world where people ate *steak au poivre* and urinated on mounds of ice cubes. I imagined myself returning to school in the fall, sitting in a classroom with all those kids. It seemed as weird as me sitting in this restaurant eating cooked snails. Either way, I'd be in the wrong place.

Where was Kelly? It had been fifteen minutes since she'd gone to the ladies' room. I hoped she wasn't sick or something.

I watched a woman eat something that looked like it used to be a small bird. She used her knife and fork delicately, removing tiny slivers of flesh from the carcass, pushing them rapidly between her bright red lips. Then I noticed Sicard staring at me, a faint smile curving his sinewy lips. He raised his gravelly voice and said, "Women troubles, kid?"

I shrugged. "Not really."

"You could fool me."

A waiter arrived at Sicard's table with a steak. I wondered if it was the *steak au poivre*. Sicard immediately snatched up his knife and fork and tore into it, jamming a huge hunk of meat into his mouth. He swallowed without chewing.

"It's good," he said, a glob of brown sauce decorating his chin. Sicard shoveled food into his mouth as if he hadn't eaten in days. He cleared his plate, wiped his mouth, belched, winked at me, then walked out of the restaurant without paying. The busboy cleared his table and set out new linen. The entire episode could not have taken more than three minutes.

I was getting more worried about Kelly. Should I go to the ladies' room and knock on the door? My *steak au poivre* arrived.

"Excuse me," I said to the waiter. "My girlfriend—she went to the rest room a long time ago and hasn't come back. I was wondering if you—if somebody—could check and see if she's okay?"

He said, his face carefully expressionless, "The young lady departed several minutes ago, sir."

"Departed?"

"In a taxi, sir."

I went numb.

"Will there be anything else, sir?"

"No. Thank you."

"Very good, sir."

I looked down at my steak, a huge, thick, heavily peppered slice of beef swimming in a pool of dark sauce, identical to the meal Sicard had just inhaled. I cut off a piece, sniffed it, and put it in my mouth.

It was the best-tasting thing I have ever eaten in my life. I ate it all, even the watercress garnish. Since I was paying for it, I wasn't going to waste a bite.

For dessert, I ordered *crème brûlée*. I ate the sweet, silky pudding slowly, savoring each creamy bite. When I finished I asked the waiter for the check.

"Your bill has been paid, sir."

"Paid?"

"The young lady took care of it, sir."

"Oh."

"Would you like me to call you a taxi, sir?"

"No thank you." I picked up the necklace and put it in my pocket. "I think I'll just crawl."

Dragon Lady raised on the flop.

Smitty and the two tourists called.

I reraised twenty.

Cookie took his unlit cigar from his mouth and wheezed, "What you eat f'dinna, kid? Railroad spikes?"

"Yeah, about twenty miles worth."

Cookie gave out a wet chortle. "I fold," he said.

Dragon Lady called.

Smitty folded.

The tourists both called.

I smiled. My lips felt tight against my teeth.

"Let's see some more cards," I said.

The dealer dealt.

PART THREE
AUGUST

COOKIE

I watched the speedometer climb to 80, 90, 95. The road stretched out across the prairie, open and clean. Wind tore at my hair. 100, 105, 110. It hit me then, the feeling like I had a great hand in a big pot. I let the feeling ride, then eased off on the accelerator and let the Camaro drift back down to 85, along with my heartbeat. Cruising speed.

The odometer read 979.

I'd had the car for three days.

At mile post 273 I exited the freeway and followed River Road north, taking the curves as fast as I dared, hearing the tires moan as they strained to grip the asphalt.

"Pretty cool, huh?" I said, turning to look toward the passenger seat. I could see the wind whipping her red-blond hair. I could see her smile, and that wild sparkle in her bright blue eyes. But Kelly was not part of my life anymore.

The passenger seat was empty.

I'd tried to call her a few times. All she'd said was, "Denn, I'm sorry, but I can't be with you anymore. I care about you. I really do. But we aren't good for each other right now. Maybe we can be friends sometime, but not now. We need to be apart."

"Maybe you need to be apart, but what about me?"

She wouldn't even talk about it. I even went over there once and talked to her mother. Mrs. Rollingate was polite and cold. I could tell she felt sorry for me, but I could also tell that nothing I said would make any difference.

Too bad for Kelly Rollingate. She was missing out.

I downshifted and punched it, getting rubber in fourth gear.

I drove the River Road all the way up to Benson, crossed at the bridge, took County 19 back to the freeway, driving slower now, beeping the horn at a couple of kids on bicycles.

I got off at Addison Avenue and cruised through downtown. I saw Murky trimming the arbor vitae in front of the Chatham Arms apartment building. I beeped and waved. Murky looked up, watching expressionlessly as I rolled by.

Me in my new car.

Since I wasn't seeing Kelly anymore, I was spending more time at the casino. My poker game was better than ever. Before, I'd been a passive player, reading the other players, knowing the odds, taking their money when I had the cards. But after Kelly left me, something inside went cold and hard and clear. I found myself playing aggressively, controlling the action, master of the poker table, taking the game where I wanted it to go—straight into my pocket.

I had moved up to the forty-dollar-limit game, the biggest game offered at the Hand. A lot of the regulars wouldn't play against me anymore, but there were plenty of tourists to go around.

And then there was Cookie Green.

Cookie, I had learned, was a "prop." He worked for the casino. His job was to sit in on games when there weren't enough players to make a full table. He played with his own money, but he was also paid by the casino to make himself available. In short, he played cards for a living. And he was good at it.

I couldn't beat him.

But, then, he couldn't beat me, either. We respected each other, and almost every night we tried to win each other's money.

One night I was sitting at the casino bar drinking a Coke, waiting for a game to get started, when Cookie took the stool next to me and ordered a glass of milk.

"How's it going, Swanee?" he wheezed. Cookie was the unhealthiest-looking human being I'd ever seen outside a hospital. His skin looked like yellowed paper covered with cracked white paste, his wheezy breathing was audible from across a card table, his false teeth made a clacking noise when he spoke, and his hands shook so bad, he sometimes had to grab one with the other to keep them still. Sometimes, in the middle of a hand, he would put on a pair of glasses thick as a deck of cards and peer at the cards with a slack-jawed expression, as if he did not know where he was or what he was doing. When he walked, he moved slowly, his back bent, watching the carpet for anything that might trip him and break his brittle bones.

Players who didn't know Cookie fell for the whole shtick. Since he was so obviously on his way to the next world, they didn't like to raise him or call his bets. Cookie took their money with his shaking hands and thanked them wheezily.

It was all an act. I'd once seen Cookie on the street downtown walking straight and tall.

He'd stopped at a newsstand and asked for a copy of *The Racing Form*, a daily paper devoted to horse racing. His voice had been deep and clear, and the tremor in his hands had not appeared. He walked off, reading *The Racing Form*, without his glasses.

The only part of his decrepitude that was real was that awful complexion.

I said, "Pretty good. I'm doing okay."

"I'll say you are, kid. I ain't seen a run of luck like yours since Texas Dolly won the World Series of Poker back-to-back. Seventy-six and seven, I think it was."

"Yeah, I'm pretty lucky," I said. We both smiled, knowing that luck had nothing to do with it.

"You ever play any no-limit?"

I said, "Not lately." I'd never played no-limit, but I didn't want to admit that to Cookie.

"You'd be good at it. This limit poker, there's only so far you can go with it."

"I'd have to drive out to Las Vegas to find a no-limit game, wouldn't I?"

"Oh, there's games 'round here."

"You mean like the one at Marcel's?"

Cookie laughed, a liquid chortle that sounded like something between a death rattle and a cough. "You know about that? Let me tell you, kid, back when Marcel owned the joint I use to play every week. Use to win. I don't got the stomach for it no more. A guy like you, though, a guy like you could beat that game. Artie Kingston wouldn't scare a guy like you."

"The King?"

Cookie nodded. "They call him that now, don't they? Twenty years ago little Artie use to be a punk kid, then he got this idea he could play cards, and he was right. He won the restaurant off Marcel a couple years back. Poor Marcel has four kings, draw poker, and Artie Kingston rolls up a straight flush. Just like in the movies, Swanee. I seen it with my own eyes."

"Is the game rigged?"

"Nah. Artie, he don't have to cheat. He's what you call stone cold. I seen him call a ten-thousand-dollar raise easy as most guys scratch their butts. With Artie Kingston, it's just another poker hand."

"You don't play there anymore?"

"Like I say, I don't got the stomach for it no more. The stress is bad for my ticker. I figure I'm gonna croak at the poker table, but I wanna put it off long as I can."

"But the game is straight?"

"Sure it is." Cookie shrugged. "A kid plays

like you, you could beat that game. You got to be stone cold, though. You remember Tic-Tac?"

Tic-Tac had been a regular at The Magic Hand. "I haven't seen him around lately."

"Artie busted him out good. Tic-Tac's in a program now."

"Program?"

"Yeah, he give up gambling. Now he's in GA. Gamblers Anonymous. Anyways, Artie don't even really care how much he wins, long as at the end of the night somebody gets into him for a few thousand. He wants his dime a week."

"Ten percent a week?"

"He borrow you a thousand, the vigorish is a hundred a week. His man Sicard handles the loans for him. That's Artie's main business. Only reason he got that restaurant's 'cause Marcel got into him too deep and then made that play with his four no-good kings. Artie, he fancies himself a class act, but he's just another loan shark. Cards is just a way how he makes it happen. That's what cards is, y'know, Swanee. Cards is a doorway to get you where you want to be."

I said, "Huh?"

He touched his forehead. "There's you here." He pointed out across the casino floor.

"Then there's life out there." He held up his papery hands, making a frame with thumbs and forefingers, looking through the frame at me. "Then there's how you connect to it, Swanee. You get to it through the cards. Cards is real, Swanee. The cards keep on coming, every hand different. Like opening doors, Swanee."

His hands fell to his lap, and for a moment Cookie's eyes went vacant. He blinked, saw the half-empty glass of milk sitting on the bar before him. He drank the milk. "Every door's different, kid. Just keep 'em coming. Sooner or later you get the one you been waitin' for."

TEETH

I ran into Sam Grant at Wager's Drive-in. I was sitting in my Camaro working my way through the Super Cheeseburger Basket when Sam and his girlfriend, Rita, pulled in next to me.

"Hey there, Sam," I said, raising my sunglasses so he would recognize me.

Sam, startled, looked from me to my car, then back at me. "Nice ride," he said.

"It gets me around."

"Yeah, I bet it does. Hey, you hear about Hicks?"

"Jason? Uh-uh." I shoved some fries into my mouth.

"He's in jail," Sam said. "Him and Gibby both."

My mouth full of fries, I could only chew and stare back at him.

Sam said, "Middle of the night, him and Gibby cleaned out the Amoco where Jason

♠ 139 ♦

was working, loaded all the tools and stuff in Gibby's van and drove it over to Springfield and tried to sell it to this auto body shop down there."

I swallowed. "They're in *jail*?" It didn't seem real.

"The body shop guy called the cops on 'em."

Rita leaned over Sam and said, "Hey, are you Dennis Doyle?"

"Yeah, that's me."

"How come you didn't tell me this was Dennis Doyle?" she whined at Sam.

"I thought you knew him."

"Well, I don't. Hey, Dennis Doyle, I got a girlfriend wants to meet you. She thinks you're cool."

"Sorry, I'm not in the market," I said. "I don't have time for women these days."

She drew back. "Yeah, I heard you were kind of a jerk."

Maybe I *was* a jerk, but it was true what I'd said. Girls were a distraction. I was better off without them. In fact, I was better off without a lot of people. My life had gotten a lot simpler now that Kelly was history and Murky wasn't hanging around stuffing food in his face and yapping at me and I didn't have to deal with any lawn customers. I was spending almost all my time in three places: the casino, my car, and my room.

I decided to stop off at the third place before going to the first place.

The sound of Neil Diamond and the smell of fresh-baked corn bread filled the house. A suitcase stood beside the front door. I turned off the stereo and went into the kitchen. My mom was adding chopped tomatoes to a pot of chili—one of my favorite meals. She made chili the way I liked it best, with chopped beef-steak and chili peppers and fresh tomatoes and spices. No onions, no beans.

She looked at me and smiled really hard. "You don't like Neil Diamond?" she said, stir-ring the tomatoes into the pot.

"It was too loud," I said. "You keep listen-ing to that nasty rock and roll and you'll be deaf before you're forty."

"Then I guess we'll have to learn sign lan-guage." We both laughed—it was an old joke between us.

I remembered that it was Friday, the day I always got an envelope full of "mystery" cash in the mail.

"Did I get any mail today?"

"Just some catalogs and the gas bill, dear. There was nothing for you."

I nodded. As I'd suspected, the money had been coming from Jason.

"So what's with the suitcase?" I asked. "You going someplace?"

Mom raised her eyebrows. "Me? No. I packed the suitcase for you, honey. Your plane leaves tonight at nine."

Plane? I'd completely forgotten about going to LA. I'd blocked it out of my mind like a bad dream. I said, "Oh. I'm supposed to go see Fred, aren't I?"

"Aren't you excited?" she said.

I felt like throwing up. I said, "I'm not going. I have to work tonight."

My mom's mouth opened into a perfect circle, but nothing came out. We stared at each other for an eternity. It felt as if a thick rubber band were stretching between us.

I let go first. I ran out the front door and jumped in my car.

The International Association of Orthodontic Surgeons was in town, and every table at the Hand was full. I sat in the lounge for nearly an hour waiting for a seat, thinking about Jason Hicks paying me off sixty dollars at a time. What had driven him to steal all that equipment from the Amoco station? Had Gibby talked him into it? Or was Jason still was Jason still deep in debt to Kingston?

Finally, a seat opened up in the ten-twenty hold 'em game. Except for Dragon Lady, all of the players were new faces. They all had very white, very even teeth. Dragon Lady was cleaning up. She must've had five thousand dollars in front of her.

Those orthodontists had perfect teeth, but they were all terrible poker players.

Every poker game has an ebb and flow. The cards run good for a while, then they run bad. Sometimes the action is fast and loose, then the players calm down and play their cards tight and close. There are periods when everybody is talking and laughing, followed by spells of relative quiet. When I'm playing good I get into a groove. I look at my cards. Pair of deuces? I fold. Decisions become automatic. Aces? I raise. My mind spins off. I see myself driving down a highway, taking the curves fast, but always in control.

I could read those perfect teeth like traffic signals. A hundred hands with the orthodondists had put me up two thousand dollars. Every time one set of teeth busted out, another would appear to take his place.

A tall man with hair and flesh the color of

beach sand took an empty seat across from me. He looked familiar, but I couldn't place him. I watched as he took his cards, bet, folded, raised. His fingers were long and perfectly manicured, he wore no watch or jewelry. His face looked sculpted from cold stone. He had pale gray eyes, a thin mouth, a razor-sharp nose. At first I thought he had no eyebrows, but then I saw their faint arch, the exact sandy color of his skin. He played cautiously, giving away nothing—no emotion, no feelings, no reactions. If anything, he appeared to be slightly bored.

I could not find the slightest hint of a tell. It was as if there were nothing inside his icy shell. Then I saw his mouth curve up and open slightly as he raked in a pot, and I remembered that flat, mouth-only smile. His teeth were crowded and slightly yellow. The last time I saw this man he had been wearing a tuxedo, greeting the customers at Marcel's.

I did not bet against him and he did not bet against me. We watched each other like two lions feeding on the same gazelle. The orthodontists paid and paid.

The sand-colored man easily won a few hundred dollars, then stood up to leave. As he passed behind my chair he leaned over and said, "You ever want to play some real poker, you give me a call."

I turned my head but he was gone, swallowed by the crowded casino.

I asked Dragon Lady, "Who was that?"

"You don't know? That was the King," she said.

"Kingston?"

"You got it, Swanee. I raise you twenty."

Kingston's seat was filled by another player. I was back on that highway, reraising a set of teeth who thought his straight could beat me. Coming up over the top of a mountain pass, cruise control set at eighty, I raised him again and then showed him my full house. White teeth glared in the lights.

Dragon Lady started losing her stack and decided to cash in. It was just me and the orthodontists now. One of them said to me, "You have nice teeth." I grinned and raised his bet.

The cards kept coming. They all wanted to give me their money. The orthodontist across from me busted out. A new player took his seat. Another tall man. For a moment I thought that the King had returned, but this man was wearing a watch, and his hands were suntanned. I got dealt a pair of kings. I bet twenty. The new player just sat there, his hands resting on his cards. I lifted my eyes to look at his face. He was staring right at me. The world seemed to tilt. I was not looking at another poker player.

I was looking at my father.

GRIZZLY

Fred helped me carry my chips to the glass-fronted cashier cage. He watched silently as she counted out my money. I was in a dream. The floor felt spongy. Everything was in supersharp focus.

"Good cards?" he asked.

"Not really," I said. "Orthodontists."

"Yeah, I had a hard time finding a hotel room. I never saw so many straight teeth in all my life. Not even in Hollywood."

Maybe this *was* a dream. Maybe I was asleep on my feet. Maybe I was still sitting at the hold 'em table, winning.

The cashier finished her count. "Ten thousand three hundred dollars," she said, pushing a thick sheaf of hundred-dollar bills through the opening in the glass. I picked up the money and riffled through it. I looked at Fred.

"Not bad for a few hours work, eh?"

Fred frowned. "A few hours? Denn, do you know how long you've been here?"

I shrugged. I don't keep track of time when I'm winning.

"What do you think I'm doing here?" he said.

"I dunno." I felt confused. What *was* he doing there? Wasn't he supposed to be in LA? Fred was leading me out of the casino. It was dark. "What time is it?" I asked.

"Eleven-thirty."

That wasn't so bad. I'd only been playing since six. But I *felt* like I'd been playing all night long.

He said, "Your mother called me, sport. She was pretty worried about you. I came as soon as I could."

"You must've jumped right on a plane. I don't see what's the big deal. I was gonna call you in the morning. I told her I had to work tonight."

"Tonight?" Fred sighed and squeezed my shoulder. "Denn, Denn. That was yesterday, sport. You've been here for more than twenty-four hours."

Fred wouldn't let me drive.

"You're spaced out, sport. Asleep on your feet. We can come pick up your car tomorrow." He led me to his rental car, a big white Lincoln. "Right now I want to get you home to your mother. She's been practically out of her mind worrying about you."

I was still in shock from finding out I'd been playing poker for almost thirty hours straight. But the wad of hundred-dollar bills in my jeans pocket felt great.

I said, "I told her I was going to the casino."

"She called, champ. Several times. She even drove out here once. But nobody'd ever heard of a Dennis Doyle. What is it they call you?"

"Swanee."

"What's that about?"

"Nothing. She actually came out to the casino?"

"Yeah, but she was looking for a kid emptying ashtrays, not a gambler at the twenty-dollar limit hold 'em table. I almost didn't recognize you myself. That's high stakes, sport."

"I always win," I mumbled. The hours at the card table were catching up fast. I could feel the fatigue gathering around me like a cold, fuzzy cocoon. We were moving fast now, the dashes on the road flashing hypnotically. A large moth spattered against the windshield.

Fred said, "Denn?"

"Hmm?"

"I want you to know that I understand. Sometimes when you're good at something you just can't leave it alone. You just have to chase it. But when you catch it, Denn, it maybe turns out to be a big old grizzly bear. Denn? Are you with me, champ?"

"You caught a bear?"

I heard him chuckle.

"Yeah, I think maybe we both got hold of one, sport. You and me both."

I vaguely remember getting home and my mom being all over me and trying to feed me, and then I was in my own bed, asleep.

I slept until one-thirty the next afternoon. When I woke up I lay in bed staring at the ceiling. I wasn't looking forward to seeing my mom, but I was so hungry, I could feel my stomach twisting around itself, crying for food. Maybe she wasn't home. I put on a pair of jeans and headed for the kitchen.

I never got there.

They were waiting for me in the living room.

My mom was sunk into the sofa, Fred holding her hand.

I scanned their unsmiling faces. I didn't know what they had in mind, but whatever it was, they weren't bluffing.

* * *

My first weird thought, seeing their hands all twisted together like that, was that they were going to get married again. The thought of it gave me a moment of false joy, and then I felt like throwing up. I knew it would never happen. Fred could no more return to my mother than I could go back to mowing lawns. Our family would never be together again.

So why were they sitting there shoulder-to-shoulder, looking at me?

Fred said, "Denn, would you sit down a moment, please?"

"What's the matter?" Had somebody died? Maybe one of them had cancer. I didn't want to sit down until I knew which way the wind was blowing. Fred's face had gone blank, like a poker player with a huge hand. My mother looked as if she might shatter at the slightest touch.

"Just sit down, Denn."

I sat.

"Denn," he said, "your mother and I are worried about you."

I should've known. It was about the one and only thing in this world that mattered to all three of us. Me. Dennis Doyle.

What had them worried was the one part

of my life that was going perfect. They were worried about me playing poker. How ironic.

It wasn't healthy, they said. I was underage. I was neglecting my household chores. I was turning away from my friends and family. They'd heard that I was going to quit school in the fall. They thought I had a "gambling problem."

"I don't get it," I said. "What's the problem if I'm winning?"

I sat and listened as my father talked, and then my mom talked, and then my mom cried. It went on for a while without either of them making much sense. Then the phone rang. Fred jumped up and said he was expecting an important call. He disappeared into the kitchen for ten minutes while Mom and I sat and stared at each other's feet.

When Fred came back I was ready for him.

I said, "So what do you want?"

"We want you to be happy, Denn," said my mother.

"We want you to finish school," said my father.

"Okay." I made my play. "I'll go to school in the fall. I'll make sure to take care of things around the house. I'll come home every night before midnight."

Fred shook his head. "No more casino, sport. You're only sixteen."

My mom said, "We think you should spend a few weeks with your father, Denn."

Fred held up a hand.

"Uh, small change of plan there, Sally. That call I just got? That was the studio. I have to fly up to Montana; don't know for how long. Steven wants all the writers on the set during the filming. Script problems, you know. I really have to be there."

My mom looked a bit stunned. I almost smiled, watching their game plan collapse.

Fred gave my mom a pitying look, then said to me, "Denn, this isn't a negotiation. The casino is off-limits, and you *will* return to school. Once you turn eighteen you can do what you want, but for now you have to follow a few rules. Understand?"

I understood. I didn't buy it, but I understood.

"And I want you to go talk to Father O'Gara."

Whoa! Where did *that* come from? "What for?" I asked.

"Because I'm not going to be here, and because I know Seamus O'Gara and he knows you, and I think it will do you good to talk to him." Fred looked at his watch. "Look, I've got to catch a flight." He looked at my mom. "I'm sorry, Sally. This is really important."

She nodded resignedly.

I said, "Maybe Seamus doesn't want to talk to me."

"He's expecting you, sport."

Now I understood. We weren't playing poker anymore; this was football. Fred had just executed a handoff.

RED WINE

Seamus, dressed in his priest uniform, led me through the church to a little room behind the altar where he got a bottle of wine out of the small refrigerator.

"Come on," he said, leading me down a short hallway to his office.

I'd never been in his office before. It was a mess.

"You opening a bookstore?" I asked. I was only half kidding. He must've had a thousand books and just as many magazines. The shelves were stuffed, and several cardboard boxes, overflowing with books and magazines, lined one wall. The titles I could see were mostly religious or philosophical, with a few books about running scattered among them.

Seamus said, "I read a lot." He sat down behind his desk and set the bottle of wine beside his telephone. He gestured at a chair that was holding up about five years' worth of *Runner's World*. "Have a seat."

I picked up the stack of magazines, set them on the floor, and sat down.

"Okay," I said. "I'm here."

"Yes, you are," Seamus said. "So . . . you're a poker player, I hear."

"Look, Seamus—"

He held up a hand. "Denn, I want you to call me Father, or Father O'Gara."

I smiled, thinking he was kidding, but one good look at his face cured me of that. Seamus was serious. "How about if I call you 'Reverend,'" I said. "I mean, you aren't my father."

"Reverend will do, for now."

"Okay then, Rev, there's something you should know about me. I mean, before we get into some kind of heavy conversation." I took a breath. "See, I don't believe in God." I'd never said it out loud before, but it was true.

Seamus nodded slowly. He didn't seem at all surprised. He said, "Denn, most of the people who enter this church every Sunday don't believe in God, either. It's just not that big a deal."

You could have knocked me out with a one-dollar chip. That was the last thing I ever expected to hear from a priest—even Seamus Reverend O'Gara, the running nut.

He continued. "My guess is that only about a third of them truly believe. They might *think* they believe, but it's clear from the way they live their lives that they are fooling themselves. People don't come to church to be with God. They come here to be with other people. God's got nothing to do with it."

"You're kidding, right?"

"Not at all. It's not necessary to believe, Denn. You don't have to believe in the sun to get a sunburn, and you don't have to like bread to derive nourishment from it. Sometimes it's enough to simply go through the motions. You have to start someplace." He sat back in his chair. "Denn, what do you want out of life?"

"I don't know." I had to be careful here—I had the feeling he was setting me up, sandbagging me.

"You want to be happy, right?"

"Who doesn't?"

"What makes you happy?"

I thought about that. "I like it when things are interesting. I don't like to be bored, and I don't want people to bug me, and I want money. And I don't want to, like, be responsible for other people's screwed-up lives."

Seamus nodded. "Does poker give you that?"

"Some of it."

"Do you know why? I mean, why poker in particular, instead of, say, long-distance running, or standing on your head, or doing lawn work."

"Anybody can do lawn work. Nobody plays poker like I play poker. I'm the best."

"Is that why you play?"

"That's some more of it."

Seamus nodded and fixed his gaze on the wine bottle. After a few seconds I said, "What's the wine for?"

Seamus looked up as if surprised to find me still sitting there. "The wine?"

"Yeah. Are you gonna drink it or what?"

He shook his head. "Denn, your father asked me to talk to you about your gambling. I don't usually tell people how to live their lives, you know."

That was one of the things I'd always liked about Seamus.

"But on those rare occasions when I do, I like to remember that I am capable of messing up my own life just as bad as anybody else. Hence, the wine."

"What, you're an alcoholic?"

Seamus laughed, and his laughter had a

bitter edge. "Denn, I'm never more than a few drinks away from being an abusive, foul-mouthed, fall-down-and-crawl-in-the-gutter drunk. But I haven't had a drop in twelve years and twenty-three days." He lifted the bottle and held it up to the light. "I always loved the color of burgundy," he said softly.

"Are you saying that I'm a gambling addict?"

Seamus set the bottle gently on his desk blotter. "All I know, Denn, is that when I was drinking I was the best. Nobody knew wine like I knew wine. I even wrote a column for a wine magazine. You could give me a glass of wine and I could tell you the variety of grape, the country of origin, the region, and some-times even the year. It was an obsession. I trav-eled to France just to drink wine and visit the wineries."

"Was that before you were a priest?"

Seamus nodded. "After I quit drinking, I entered the priesthood." He laughed. "I wanted to become the best Roman Catholic priest in the world."

"You still working on that?"

"Not really. I've figured some things out in the last few years, Denn. I figured out that the more obsessed I become with wine or religion or"—he gestured at the mess in his office—

"reading or running, for that matter, the more difficult my life becomes.

"See, when I was drinking, and my whole life started to fall apart, it wasn't too hard to figure out that alcohol was the problem. I quit drinking and started going to AA meetings. It wasn't easy, but I always knew what I had to do. I had to quit drinking, period. It was bad for my mind and my body and sooner or later it would kill me. So I gave it up and decided to become the best priest in the world. I wanted to be Pope John and Mother Teresa and Jesus of Nazareth all rolled into one. I rode that obsession for about six years. It was seductive, Denn. Religion isn't bad for you. It doesn't leave you with a hangover in the morning. It doesn't give you cirrhosis of the liver. It doesn't cost you eighty dollars a bottle. The more I immersed myself in my studies, the less I could see what it was doing to me. I thought I was getting better, but in fact I was digging myself another hole. I shut out the outside world, and I even shut out the other students at the seminary. I went for almost a year without calling my folks back in Connecticut. They were a distraction, you know?"

Boy, did I ever know that one.

"Then one day I get a call from my sister

and she tells me that Dad's cancer got worse, and he was in the hospital on a respirator. I'd gotten so out of touch, I didn't even know he was sick."

"But you didn't give up being a priest."

"No. In fact, after my dad died I got more into it than ever. Then, a year later, my mother died. I still didn't get it. I was ordained, and I received a call to a little church in a little town called Drachman, where I was to help out an old monsignor named Father George Thomas Hellman. Isn't that a great name for a priest? The kids called him the Go To Hell Man, but he really wasn't like that. Father Hellman was just a very nice, very tired, very old priest who was delighted to have this relatively young new assistant at his side.

"I took on the job the way I figured Mother Teresa and Pope John would go at it. I worked so hard to bring God into the lives of the good people of Drachman, it's a miracle that Jesus Christ himself didn't drift down just to shake my hand.

"I'd been there six months when Father Hellman called me into his office and sat me down and said, 'Son, I like you a whole lot, and that's why I'm gonna shoot straight from the hip on this. You know how many folks we got showing up most Sundays?'

"'About two hundred?' I guessed.

"'More like one hundred twenty, give or take. That's about forty less than used to show up, say, six months ago. And do you know how much money we've been taking in those Sundays? Well, son, it's less every week. Nothing sorrier than a parish that can't afford to pay its electric bill.

"I said, 'Maybe we have to work harder to get people into the church.'

"Father Hellman shook his head. 'Son, what we got to do—what *you* got to do—is work *less* hard. You're scaring them off, son. Folks 'round here just aren't comfortable around all that intensity, you know what I mean?'

"Well, I didn't, and every Sunday there were a few more empty pews in church, and the collection just kept getting smaller. And the nearest Catholic church to us was thirty-two miles away, and then old Father Hellman died, bless his soul, and folks stopped coming to my church altogether. That's how I wound up here at St. Luke's. If I hadn't learned to lighten up a bit, the pews would be empty here, too. Are you with me, Denn?"

"I think so. You're telling me you used to be a jerk."

Seamus laughed. "Something like that."

"And you're telling me that I'm a jerk because I'm a good poker player."

"Not because you're good. You're a jerk because poker is the thing that matters to you the most."

"That's not true." I tried to think of other things that mattered to me. My mom mattered to me, but it had been easy to lie to her about my "job" at The Magic Hand. Kelly mattered a lot, although she was history now. Murky mattered, except he hated me. Even Fred mattered, in a way. I mean, I didn't care about him, but I cared what he thought about me. I guess I cared about Seamus in the same way. I wanted him to be proud of me. "I care about a lot of things besides poker," I said.

"Maybe," Seamus said. "But you don't care about a lot of things *more* than poker."

Seamus and I talked for a while longer. The conversation drifted to sports, then into other areas. By the time I left I had decided to give up gambling for a while, just to humor him, and to get my parents off my back. I'd give it up for a few weeks, just to see what happened. I had plenty of money, and it might not be a bad idea to go back to school. I was looking forward to driving my new car into the school lot. I was *not* looking forward to going to Gamblers Anonymous, but Seamus had insisted. There was a meeting the next Friday night in the church basement.

"Just one meeting," he said. "A couple hours. No big deal."

LOSERS

I spent most of the next few days alone, listening to music and reading and staring at my bedroom walls. Every time I left my room my mother tried to push some kind of food on me. Fred phoned a couple times, but I ducked his calls. I went for some long drives, got a couple speeding tickets, and listened to a lot of loud head-banging rock and roll. Other than talking to my mom, about the only conversation I had was with Tyler Kitterage.

Ty pulled into the Holiday station while I was gassing up my Camaro. He was driving a pickup full of rakes and shovels and other lawn-care junk. A magnetic sign on the side of the truck read S & K LAWN SERVICE.

"How's it going, Ty?" I asked him. "How's business?"

Ty had grown a beard. Either that or his face was dirty—it was hard to tell. He grinned, and the whiskers rearranged themselves. "Not too bad." He looked at my car. "Not as good as you, though. I hear you've been winning at the casino."

"Yeah, but I don't go anymore. I decided to quit while I was ahead." It felt weird to say it out loud like that. Was I really thinking about quitting? A politician might call it my "official position." I preferred to think of myself as temporarily out of action.

Ty said, "I wish Mark would quit."

For a second I didn't know who he was talking about. "Mark? You mean Murky?"

"Yeah. He likes to be called Mark now. He's been playing cards with these guys from Fulton." Fulton was the other big high school on the east side of Fairview. "He was winning for a while, but lately I think he's been losing. He borrowed a hundred bucks from me last week."

"I thought you guys were making a lot of money."

"We're doing good, Denn. That's why it was so weird that he had to borrow money."

"Yeah, well, Murky is a weird guy."

Ty laughed. "You're telling me!" He scratched his thin beard. "You think you could talk to him, Denn?"

"Me?" This was too bizarre. I was the one supposed to have a gambling problem, and here I was being asked to help Murky with his problem. "I don't think he'd listen to me, Ty. In fact, I think he doesn't want anything to do with me."

"He talks about you a lot."

"He does?"

"Yeah. I think he sort of admires you."

I called Murky that same day, just an hour before my first Gamblers Anonymous meeting. When he answered the phone I tried to pretend like nothing had ever gone sour between us.

"Hey, Murk, what's happening?"

Silence.

"Murk?"

"What?"

"I was just thinking about you, thought I'd give you a call, see how you're doing."

Silence. "I'm doing fine," he said.

I said, "So, ummm, I hear the lawn business is doing better than ever. That's really great."

Silence. "We're doing okay."

"Yeah, that's what I hear. Yep." This had to be the awkwardest conversation I'd ever had. If he "admired" me the way Ty said, he was doing a good job of hiding it. "That's really great, Murk."

"My name is *Mark*," he said.

"Oh. Okay, Mark. So, Mark, you playing any cards lately?"

"What do you want, Denn?"

"Nothing!"

"You don't ever want nothing."

He was making this hard. I said, "I hear you've been playing poker with some of those Fulton guys."

"I played a couple times."

"How'd you do?"

"Pretty good. Listen, Denn, if you're looking for a card game, we don't need any more players, okay?"

"Hey, *Mark*, I don't need a card game. As a matter of fact, I gave it up. What's the matter with you? I just call to say hello and see how you're doing and you act like a creep."

Silence. Then he said, "Look, Denn, I'm doing fine. I got my own life now. Why don't you get one?"

He didn't wait for my answer. I heard a faint click, and he was gone.

The Friday night GA group met in the basement rec room at St. Luke's, right after the Alcoholics Anonymous meeting. The room reeked of cigarettes and spilled coffee. I sat near the back and watched the anonymous gamblers filter in. What amazed me was how familiar their faces were. One time or another, I'd seen most of them at the Hand. I didn't know their names, but I'd seen them working the slots, or hunched over the blackjack table, or throwing the dice. A couple of them looked at me as they entered the room, but most of those anonymous gamblers were someplace inside themselves. They hardly noticed the kid sitting in the back row.

Tic-Tac came in just before the meeting started.

"Hey, Tic-Tac," I said.

He looked at me, gave a hollow smile, and said, "How's it going?" Without waiting for my reply, he sat down a few rows ahead of me.

I could tell he didn't even recognize me.

The meeting started with prayer, but I stayed anyway. Then one of the anonymous gamblers stood up and told about how gambling had destroyed his marriage, cost him his job, and nearly landed him in jail. When he was done, another anonymous gambler said his bit. Every story I heard ended with them losing a lot of money and getting in serious trouble. After listening to five or six of them, I left. I didn't belong in that room.

They were all a bunch of losers.

REAL

My world was shrinking.

I spent another week reading comic books, helping my mom do boring stuff around the house, or going for long drives in my Camaro. I didn't feel like doing anything else, or talking to anybody, or anything. I stuck by my promise to Fred and my mom and Seamus and stayed away from the casino. It wasn't hard at all. It was just incredibly boring. I thought about calling Murky to tell him how bored I was, but I didn't think he'd appreciate it.

My mom was walking on eggs. Every whiny sentence started out, "Denn, honey, would you . . . ?"

Would I what? Would I take out the trash, would I like a grilled cheese sandwich, would I mind moving my feet so she could finish sweeping the kitchen floor, would I open this jar . . . ? Sure I would. I'd do anything she asked. I was the perfect son. I didn't drink, smoke, gamble, or bring strange women into the house.

"Denn, honey, would you answer the phone, please?"

I picked up the extension.

"How's it going, Denn?" It was Seamus. He sounded a little out of breath.

"Hey, Rev," I said. "You sound winded."

"Just got in from a run. Whew! I've got to get my miles in—I'm running back-to-back 10Ks next weekend."

"How far did you run today?"

"Fifteen miles."

"Isn't that sort of *obsessive?*" I said.

Seamus laughed. "Maybe it is. So, Denn, are you coming to the GA meeting tonight?"

"I don't know." There was no way I was going to that thing again. "I might just stay home tonight. But, don't worry—I'm not going to run out and start playing cards."

He said, "That's not what this is about, Denn."

"Yes it is. If I was into long-distance running or studying astronomy or fishing or any of the other activities on your 'approved by God and most parents' list, you all wouldn't be on my case. But since I'm only sixteen years old and you and my folks don't want me to play poker, I guess I won't be playing any poker for a while. I keep my promises. But there's something you guys don't get at all. You keep talking about gambling. I don't gamble. I never have. You'd never catch me dumping quarters in a slot machine or betting a roulette number or buying a lottery ticket. I play poker. Or, anyways, I used to. Poker is a game of skill, and I happen to be good at it."

"Denn, I thought we talked about that. You can be a winner at cards and still lose at life."

"Or you can be a winner all around. You want to know something else? The people at that GA meeting? They didn't get it, either. They weren't talking about poker. They weren't even talking about gambling. They talked about two things the whole time I was there. They talked about losing, and they talked about addiction. I don't have a problem with either of those things."

"Denn—"

I heard a click: Call Waiting. "I've got another call coming in, *Rev*, I'll have to call you back later. I hit the flash button. "Hello?"

"Hey, sport, How you doing?"

"Hi, Fred. I'm fine. Did you want to talk to Mom?"

"I just called to see how you were doing on the new program."

"What program is that?"

"Don't shine me on, champ. Are you staying away from that casino?"

"Yeah."

"Good! You doing okay money-wise?"

"I've got some money. I'm not a loser, Fred."

"Hey, I never said you were. How much money did you win there, anyway?"

"You mean the night you dragged me out of there? Ten thou."

"I mean all together."

I did some quick math. There was the money I had in the bank, plus the cash in my dresser drawer, plus the money I'd spent on my car, and the insurance, and the money for Kelly's necklace—I'd never returned it—and my new computer and a few other things I'd bought.

"Around fifty thousand," I said.

His breath hissed into the phone. He said, "Wow. I can see why you didn't want to give it up."

"It's no big deal," I said. What I didn't tell Fred, and what I hadn't told Seamus or anybody else, was that playing poker, for me, was not about the money and winning anymore. Something had changed, and maybe it was me. Money and winning were important, sure, but they weren't what kept me awake at night.

It was the action, the ebb and flow of fate, the expressions on the faces of the players, the sounds and smells of the casino. But most of all it was the cards.

I missed the hiss of a fresh new deck being spread across green felt. The magic moment when my hand touched the slick backs of the cards, my thumb lifted the corners just enough to reveal to me their suits and ranks. It was about cards, about every new hand delivering fresh new hope. That was what I missed the most. I understood now what Cookie had meant:

Cards is real, Swanee. The cards keep on coming, every hand different. Like opening doors, Swanee. . . . Every door's different, kid. Just keep 'em coming. Sooner or later you get the one you been waitin' for.

WHEELS

Nothing days faded into meaningless nights. I actually missed mowing lawns. At one point I got so bored, I actually drove out to the wheelchair camp at Lake Winonah. They don't call it a wheelchair camp, of course. The carved sign above the gate read CAMP CHALLENGE.

The driveway into the camp was a bumpy dirt road about half a mile long. Alongside the road ran a smooth asphalt path. I passed two kids maybe twelve years old racing their wheelchairs. These weren't your regular clunky wheelchairs, they were sleek racers, moving faster than most people can run. The two kids were totally intent on their race, their arms pumping like pistons.

When I pulled into the parking area by the lodge I noticed a softball game going on in a field down near the lakeshore. I was surprised to see that only the pitcher, the catcher, and the center fielder were in wheelchairs. The rest of the players were different in other ways. The first baseman had some sort of brace on his left leg. The second baseman wore a big helmet that made him look like an alien. The batter, a girl about nine or ten years old, had tiny, oddly formed arms. She had some sort of pivot device on around her waist to help her hold the bat.

About thirty people were standing or sitting behind the baselines watching. I walked toward the field, scanning the crowd for signs of Kelly's reddish-blond hair.

The pitcher swung his arm around and around in a windmill motion, then let the ball fly. The batter got her bat in front of it; the ball struck the bat and dribbled out into the infield. She took off running. There was nothing wrong with her legs—she was fast!

Both the catcher and the pitcher propelled their wheelchairs toward the ball. The catcher got there first. He spun his chair sideways, and the chair tipped him out onto the ground. He scooped the ball up and threw it with one motion. It was high. The first baseman jumped straight up, managing to get a good six inches of air beneath his good leg. He snagged the ball, but before he could land on the bag the runner tagged safe. The crowd roared. One excited voice grabbed my ear, and I spotted Kelly jumping up and down near the third baseline. I hadn't spotted her earlier because she had tucked most of her hair into a Camp Challenge baseball cap.

As I made my way toward her, I watched the catcher turn his chair upright and set the brakes. Then he slowly dragged himself into position and, with considerable difficulty, pulled himself up into the chair. I wondered why no one came forward to help him.

I came up behind Kelly. "Hey there, Spunky," I said, using a nickname I'd given her years ago but hardly ever used.

The way she jumped you'd have thought I'd jabbed her with a needle.

"Denn!"

"How's it going?"

"What are you doing here?"

I shrugged. "You look great," I said. She had turned that deep gold color that freckled people sometimes get late in the summer. Her eyes looked impossibly white and brilliant blue against her darker skin, and her face had a more sculpted look, as if she'd lost an ounce or two of baby fat from her cheeks.

She looked around nervously. "We aren't supposed to have friends visiting us here."

"So, I'm still a friend?"

She grabbed my elbow. "Come on, let's go for a walk."

I followed her to a narrow, overgrown path that followed the shoreline, scrambling to keep up, ducking under tree branches, trying not to trip on tree roots.

"Hey, slow down, would you?" I jumped over a small stream; a leafy branch slapped my face.

We emerged onto a rocky point. Kelly turned to face me, her arms crossed.

"What are you doing here, Denn?"

"I just stopped by to say hi." I gave her my best smile. "I thought maybe, you know, we could go for a walk or something. Last time we talked you said we could be friends."

Kelly's lips tightened, but I saw her eyes soften. She said, "I heard you quit going to that casino."

I nodded.

"That's good," she said. "I'm glad for you. It was making you into somebody you're not."

"Really? Who am I?" I asked.

"I don't know. I'm still trying to figure out who I am."

"You're Kelly the Spunkmeister Rollingate."

She smiled. It wasn't her best smile.

"Sometimes I envy these kids here, Denn. Every morning they get out of bed—

and for a lot of them that's not so easy—and right away they know what they have to do. They have to get dressed, get into their wheelchairs or braces or whatever, get themselves fed and so forth. Every ordinary thing throws them a challenge. Every day is a battle. They know what they have to do. They know who they are." She bit her lower lip and looked up into my eyes. "Denn, it's good to see you, but I want you to go now. Maybe we can be friends sometime, but not now. Not yet."

"Why? Are you seeing someone else?"

Kelly blinked, then looked away and to her right.

That was a tell.

I found out then that while it's painful to lose someone, it's even more painful when they are found by somebody else. Kelly had been found by one of the counselors at Camp Challenge. She wouldn't tell me his name, or tell me anything about him except that she'd started seeing him after our date at Marcel's.

I drove out of Camp Challenge with my wheels spinning, leaving behind a storm of pebbles and dust and the echo of the Camaro's throaty roar. It hadn't been the poker at all. That had just been her excuse to get rid of me.

I drove until the gas gauge read empty, then I filled it up and drove some more, leaving rubber on every corner, at every stop sign. A deer jumped out in front of me on Highway 25 and I didn't even slow down. Missed it by inches. I imagined myself legless and brain damaged, spending my days trying to get dressed and feed myself, drooling all over my shirt.

I got home a little after two A.M. My mother was waiting for me in the kitchen. Her eyes were red and puffy.

"Where were you?" she asked. She usually wasn't so blunt.

"Driving. Just driving."

"I was worried." Her eyes were watery. I could tell she was about thirty seconds away from another crying jag.

"I'm sorry."

She stood up and headed for her room. "Good night, Denn."

"G'night." I poured myself a glass of juice and sat down. A fancy-looking square envelope lay on the table. I picked it up and read the fine script on the enclosed card. A wedding invitation:

Mr. and Mrs. James C. Crutchfeld
are pleased to invite you to
celebrate the marriage
of their beloved daughter Cynthia Ann
to Frederick Steven Doyle, Jr. . . .

And I'd thought she'd been crying because
she was worried about me.

BIG BOB

I ran into Cookie Green at the G Street Grill.

Actually, I didn't run into him. I'd been hanging around the intersection of G Street and Calder Avenue most of the morning. I knew Cookie lived in the neighborhood, and I knew he bought his daily copy of *The Racing Form* at the newsstand on the corner, so I just parked down the street and waited until he came ambling down the street, bought his paper, then ducked into the little café on G Street.

Just because I couldn't play poker didn't mean I had to give up my poker friends.

He was sitting at the counter drinking a glass of foamy milk and reading his paper when I entered the café.

"Hey, Cookie!" I said.

Cookie looked at me. I could almost hear him riffling his mental Rolodex, trying to remember who I was. After a couple seconds something clicked and he said, "Swanee. How you doin', kid?" There was no trace of his wheeze.

"Not bad." I sat down on the next stool. "Just came in for some breakfast. You live around here?"

"Near enough, kid. Where you been the past couple weeks?"

"Taking some time off," I said. "I've been busy with other things. How are you doing?"

"I been doing better, kid. A lot better since you been gone." Cookie grinned, giving me a look at his full set of long yellow teeth. "You aren't planning on coming back anytime soon, I hope."

I laughed, but I wasn't sure he was kidding. "That's a popular point of view. Lately it seems like a lot of people don't want me around."

"You got to expect that, kid. A guy wins all the time, who wants to play with him?"

Now I *was* sure. He wasn't kidding.

I said, "Well, I won't be playing for a while."

"Good." Cookie took a sip of milk. "I got expenses."

The waitress stopped in front of me. "Coffee?"

"No thanks," I said, standing up. "I think I gotta go."

Cookie saluted me with his milk. "You're a hell of a card player, kid. I wish you the worst of luck."

I cruised the streets of Fairview slumped low in the driver's seat looking at the houses, the cars, the people that made up the city. A man delivering packages. That wasn't me. Another man in a long white car talking angrily into his cell phone. Not me, either. A kid on a skateboard. Used to be me. I envied him, but there was no way I could go back to being the kid I used to be. It would be like putting on an old coat. I didn't fit anymore. I drove through the northeast part of town with its boarded-up buildings and grimy warehouses. I drove down the interstate, around the south side and past the airport. I drove past The Magic Hand. The forty-foot-tall sparkling gold sign in the shape of a hand had once seemed to welcome me, but after my conversation with Cookie Green it looked like it was telling me to halt. Go away.

I turned on Cherrytree Boulevard and drove north past the big houses with perfect lawns where Fairview's doctors and lawyers and executives lived. I saw a gardener running an edger along a stone sidewalk in front of a house that looked like something out of *Gone With the Wind*.

It was Tyler Kitterage.

I pulled over to the incredibly clean curb and rolled down my window. As far as I knew, Ty was not yet a member of the *I Hate Dennis Doyle Club*.

"Hey, Ty, how's it going?"

Ty saw me and turned off the edger. He walked over to the car, wiping the sweat off his forehead with his T-shirt. "Pretty good. Kinda hot, though. You seen Mark around?"

"Murky? Nah, he doesn't want anything to do with me."

Ty looked disappointed. "Oh. He was supposed to be here a couple hours ago with the tractor. He's never late."

I remembered that about Murky. It was true. He might be goofy and sloppy and a lousy poker player, but he was always on time.

"I'm sure he'll show up," I said.

"I hope so. He's been acting kinda weird lately."

"Weird how?"

"Remember I told you how he borrowed some money from me?"

"Yeah, you said he was playing cards with some guys from Fulton."

"Right. Well, he paid me back the next day

and told me he'd won a lot of money in this other game. He said it was a great game, guys throwing money around like it was toilet paper. He wanted me to play, but I told him I'd lost enough money at cards for one lifetime. It's his business what he does, but it makes me nervous."

"What's this new game he's in?"

Ty shrugged. "Someplace down along the river. You ever hear of Marcel's?"

I could have been worried about Murky. I could have been afraid for him. Or I might have felt disdain for him getting in over his head. I suppose I might even have felt proud of him for having the guts to play with the big boys; or sorry for him because he was stupid enough to do it.

I might have had a lot of reactions, but the one I did have took me by surprise.

I was jealous.

Win or lose, smart or stupid, victor or victim, Murky was playing cards.

I took that home with me. I tried to push it deep into my gut, but it kept coming up, rising in my thoughts along with Kelly and Cookie and Seamus and the rest of my fan club. I sat at the kitchen counter drinking a glass of juice and my mom was chattering nervously. I didn't know what she was saying until she suddenly slapped her palm down hard on the counter. I jumped about an inch.

"What? What?" I said. "What's wrong?"

My mother was so meek that her slamming the counter like that was like setting off a bomb. She said, "That's what I want to know, Dennis. Have you heard a word I've said?"

"I was thinking."

"Well, he's going to be here in half an hour, so I'd appreciate it if you'd make him feel welcome."

"Here? Who?"

"You really haven't heard a word I've said, have you?"

"I guess I missed some of it."

She shook her head, exasperated. "Bob Stockman is coming over for dinner tonight. We're having roast chicken with new potatoes and fresh green beans from the farmers' market."

"Bob Stockman? From Big Bob's Sports Emporium? I thought he asked you out and you said no."

"He did and I did, but I saw him this morning at his store and I invited him to dinner."

"What were you doing at his store?" My mom was about as interested in sports as I was in knitting.

"I was buying a tennis racquet," she said.

"You don't play tennis."

She blushed. "I'm thinking of taking it up."

Big Bob Stockman showed up with his barrel chest and deep voice and iron handshake and a bouquet of roses. Our house instantly became smaller. He raved loudly about how good the roasting chicken smelled, he told my mom she looked sensational, and he wanted to be my good buddy right off the bat. Because I'd promised my mom that I'd be the good host, I let him.

We talked about skateboards. I hadn't been on my board since my encounter with Mr. Bus, but I tried to act interested. He had a new board called the Killer Bee Hivemaster, with superfast bearings and a titanium spine. It sounded interesting, if you were into that sort of thing.

The dinner was perfect, food-wise. Big Bob pretty much forgot about me and turned his attention on my mom, who he called "Sal," a nickname I knew she hated, but she kept on smiling and blinking her eyes at him and I realized with a jolt that she looked happy. It had been a long time since I'd seen her smile like that.

By the time we got to dessert it was getting

dark outside, and I was nearly paralyzed with boredom. When the phone rang I excused myself. I grabbed the phone and carried it into my room. Whoever was on the other end, I was going to talk to them.

It was Ty Kitterage.

KING'S FULL

I parked near the exit at the back of Marcel's parking lot. I could see the entrance to the restaurant straight ahead, the sparkle of moonlight on the river to the left, and the dark bulk of the restaurant building trailing off to the right. Somewhere within that sprawling structure was a room with a card table and a lot of money changing hands.

I sat listening to the faint pops and crackles of the Camaro engine cooling, trying to get myself psyched.

Ty had been frantic on the phone.

The first thing he'd said was, "Denn, I think Mark's in some kind of trouble."

I'd said, "Oh? What did he do?"

"He never showed up at our job today. His mother said he'd just been there, but he'd gone to the bank. I was pretty mad, so I called my sister Kathy—she works at the bank—to see if I could catch him there, but he'd already come and gone. You know what she told me? She said Murky had withdrawn all the money in our business account except ten bucks. We had almost four thousand dollars in there, Denn."

"Ty, I don't get why you're telling me this."

"You're his friend, aren't you?"

"Like I told you before, he doesn't want anything to do with me."

"Well, I don't know what I'm supposed to do. You think I should call the cops or what?"

"You think he stole the money?"

Ty didn't say anything right away. Then he said, "I think he took it to that poker game at Marcel's."

"Maybe he'll get lucky."

"Yeah, right. I think I *will* call the cops."

"Uh, maybe you should hold off on that, Ty. What if Murky *is* in that poker game? What if he's winning? The cops barge in, confiscate all the money, where's that leave you?"

"I didn't think of that. But I gotta do something!"

I heard Big Bob's booming laugh from the dining room.

I said, "Tell you what. How about if I drive out there, check it out?"

So that's what I did. I sat in my car for

about twenty minutes, then got out and went looking for Marcel's infamous no-limit poker room.

Jason had told me that the card room had a private entrance. I walked around the restaurant. The building looked very classy from the front, but in back it showed itself to be a weathered, wooden building that had been added onto again and again, a series of garage-sized additions that made it look like a freight train that had stopped too quickly. The first door I came to led into the kitchen—I could hear the clanking of pans and the voices of the cooks. The next two doors looked dark and unused. The last door was in back, at the far end of the building. A small wooden sign read, KING'S FULL.

I knocked, and when no one answered I tried turning the knob. The door swung inward, revealing a small, dimly lit foyer containing a sofa, two chairs, a coffee table covered with magazines, and the faint odor of cigar smoke. I stepped inside. The door opposite me opened. I could hear voices and the clatter of chips. The cigar smell intensified.

Mr. Sicard stepped into the foyer and closed the door behind him. A thick cigar jutted from his muscled lips.

"Hey, kid, how ya doing?" he said, making

it sound as if we were long-lost friends. His bright orange shirt nearly blinded me. "What can I do for ya?" He raised his short dark eyebrows, waiting for my answer. I wasn't sure what he wanted to hear, but I *was* sure that if I gave him the wrong response, he'd hustle me out of there in a second. I considered telling him that Murky had invited me, but that might not cut it, and besides, Murky would deny it in a second.

I said, "Mr. Kingston said I should stop by. Is he here tonight?"

Sicard's smile broadened, and he relaxed. He opened the door wide. "Come on in!"

I entered a clean, brightly lit room with new carpeting, a bar at one end, a couple of slot machines, a long leather sofa against one wall, and paintings of dogs playing poker decorating the paneled walls. In the center of the room was an oval, casino-type poker table. A man wearing a bow tie and a vest sat in the dealer's seat. He looked up as I entered the room and winked. It was Chuckie, one of the dealers from The Magic Hand.

Six players sat at the table. I saw Murky right away, sitting to the dealer's left, gaping at me as if I'd stepped out of a flying saucer. Kingston had his back to me, but I recognized his long neck, his narrow shoulders, and his sandy hair.

Sicard said, "I got a friend a yours here, Mr. Kingston."

Kingston turned his head slowly without moving his shoulders. As soon as his eyes found me, his head stopped turning. I could see the right half of his face. He said, "Hey there, kid." His voice was flat and machinelike.

Sicard said, "Three seats open, you can take your pick."

"How about if I just watch a few hands," I said.

Kingston returned his attention to his cards as if I no longer existed.

Sicard said, "Whateva."

I asked him what the chips were worth.

"Reds five, blues ten, blacks a hundred, grays a thou," he said.

"I'll go twenty," said the man to Sicard's left. His head looked like a russet potato.

"Up forty," wheezed the next player.

I did a double take. I hadn't noticed him sitting there.

I said, "Hey, Cookie, how's it going?"

"Not too bad, kid," he grinned, his chin hidden behind an enormous stack of chips. "We been expecting you."

* * *

I sat on the leather sofa and watched the game. Sicard sat at the other end, paring his nails with a Swiss Army knife. I tried to get a sense for who the winners and losers were. Kingston had about twenty thousand, but that didn't mean much. He might have bought more chips to start. Murky had a couple thousand dollars in front of him. If he'd brought four thousand to the game, that meant he was stuck for two grand so far.

Chuckie shuffled and dealt a new hand. They were playing hold 'em: two cards to each player, then three cards turned faceup, then two more cards faceup, one at a time.

Murky bet twenty. The two guys to his left—I thought of them as "Big Bear" and "Teddy Bear" because they both had gray beards and scowly expressions—both folded. Kingston raised forty. Potato-head folded, as did Cookie.

Murky raised eighty.

Kingston, without the slightest flicker of expression, threw his cards away. Murky eagerly swept in the pot.

I thought, Not a bad play, Murkster. But you're outclassed.

The action was slower than I was used to. The players took more time to think. Many of the pots were small, only a couple hundred dollars, and were won without a showdown—the winning hand never displayed because every player but one dropped out. I watched for half an hour before a big hand went down.

The three players at the showdown were Kingston, Potato-head, and Big Bear. Teddy Bear had folded and was pumping quarters into the slot machine. Big Bear was trying so hard to act bored, I knew he had a good hand. Potato-head looked like a man on his way to the electric chair. Kingston gave away nothing.

All the up-cards were out: two jacks, a ten, a deuce, and a king. On the final betting round, Big Bear opened for five hundred, Kingston raised another five. Potato-head sighed and put in his thousand dollars. He had decided to see the hand through, but I could see he'd already given up on it.

Big Bear looked at his cards—you could almost hear the sweat hissing from his pores—and raised again. Kingston reraised—this time a thousand dollars. Potato-head finally saw the light and dropped out.

Big Bear pushed all his chips toward the center of the table. A rivulet of sweat ran down the precise center of his forehead and gathered at the bridge of his nose. He was scared, but he thought he was going to win.

"I'm all-in," he said, counting his chips. "Two thousand two hundred forty."

Without visible emotion, Kingston matched Big Bear's bet. "Call," he said.

Big Bear turned up his concealed cards: two kings, giving him a full house—three kings over two jacks.

"Only one hand can beat me," he growled, leaning forward so far a drop of sweat fell from the tip of his nose onto the chips.

Kingston turned his concealed cards faceup: two jacks. With the two jacks already on the board, it made four-of-a-kind, the only hand that could have beat Big Bear's full house.

Big Bear's eyes bugged out. He slammed his meaty fist on the table, making everybody's chips jump, then unleashed a stream of insults and obscenities at Kingston, calling him every kind of cheat and deviant imaginable. Kingston sat quietly stacking his chips, letting the big man's words roll off him.

Sicard said, "Be nice now, big guy, you want to come back, doncha?"

"This ain't how we play cards in St. Louis," Big Bear shouted.

Kingston said in a quiet voice, "You're not in St. Louis, mister."

Big Bear suddenly deflated. His shoulders sagged, and his eyes went dead. He pushed his chair back and thumped out of the room without another word.

"Y'all come back now," Sicard called after him.

For a few seconds the room was quiet. Then Sicard turned to me and said, "Why don't you siddown, kid? They could use another player."

I drew a shaky breath. "I didn't come here to play," I said.

Kingston turned to look at me. He asked, "Why you wasting my time?"

I stood up, looking at Murky. "I came to give my friend a ride home."

Murky's mouth fell open. "What? No way, José. I'm not going anywhere."

I tried to think of something I could say or do that would convince Murky to leave with me. I could tell him he was about to lose the rest of his money, but he wouldn't believe it. I could say that Ty was going to call the police, but I could see in Murk's face that he was too far gone to care.

I said, "Murk, we were friends for a long time."

"Yeah, but that was before you started acting like a jerk."

"Maybe I did. But how about if you just do this one thing for me. Leave here now, with me. That's all I'm asking."

He thought about it. For about one entire second.

Teddy Bear said to me, "Hey, kid, you trying to break up our game? You don't wanna play, get lost!"

Murky said, "That's right, Doylie. Get lost. Go home."

I felt my face go hot and red. A hand grasped my elbow and squeezed hard. Sicard said quietly in my ear, "I think you best leave, son."

I shook loose his grip and sat down at the table. The chair was still warm from Big Bear's rear end. I pulled out a roll of hundreds and slapped it on the table.

"Deal me in," I said.

RAGS

When I picked up my first two cards my hands were shaking so hard I was afraid they would detach themselves at my wrists. I heard voices as if from far away, then felt a hand touch my elbow.

"Hey kid, whatsamatta, you having a seizure?" It was Teddy Bear's hairy face, frowning at me. The more I looked at him, the more he looked to me like a small gray bear with wire-rimmed glasses.

"I'm fine," I said.

"Well, it's your bet."

I looked at my quivering cards. Pair of eights. I checked. Kingston and Potato-head and Cookie checked, too. Murky bet forty. Teddy Bear folded. I folded. Kingston folded. Potato-head called. Cookie raised.

Murky reconsidered his cards.

I said, "You're holding losers, Murk." I knew Cookie wouldn't raise without the cards to back it up.

Teddy Bear growled, "No table talk, son."

"That's right, kid," said Sicard. "You're outta the hand, you keep your mouth out of it, too."

Murky called Cookie's raise. I sighed and watched the hand play out. Cookie won it with trip aces—one on the board, and the two in his hand.

After a few hands I calmed down. My hands steadied, and my mind focused. I went after a small pot with an ace, king in my hand, but lost it to Teddy Bear, who backed into a small straight. Mostly I just watched, waiting for the good hands, learning to read the opposition.

Potato-head, Teddy Bear, and Murky were easy.

Teddy Bear had a vein in his forehead that pulsed crazily when he liked his cards. Potato-head always made some comment about his cards when they were good. He would say, "I had this hand an hour ago," or, "My mama would *love* these cards," or, "I got me a hand." It didn't matter exactly *what* he said—if it was about his cards, the cards were good, but if he didn't like them he would remark on the weather or complain about Sicard's cigar smoke.

Murky wasn't as transparent as he used to

be, but he had his share of tells. He sat up straighter when he intended to go after a pot, and when he was bluffing he laughed a lot. When his hand was good he moved real slow, almost as if he were underwater.

Cookie was tougher to read, but I'd played against him enough to pick up his very few, very subtle tells. The most useful was his wheeze, which became slightly louder when he held a powerful hand.

Kingston was a blank. The only thing I could figure out was that when he stayed in a hand, he fully expected to win it. But that was true of all of us. We all expected to win, or we wouldn't be there. One thing surprised me, though. I'd thought that Kingston was an older guy, maybe in his fifties, but now that I was looking at him up close I could see he was younger, not a day over thirty.

Of course, I hadn't come here to play cards. I'd come to save my friend Murky from his self-destructive ways. I really had no choice but to sit down and risk my money—the six grand I just happened to have in my pocket.

I was sure my parents would understand. Seamus would understand. This wasn't about gambling, or about poker. It was about friendship.

* * *

Potato-head went all-in on a jack-high flush. I busted him with a better flush, putting me up a few thousand. Two hands later, Kingston bluffed Cookie out of a nice pot, then busted him the very next hand with a little pair of tens.

Cookie stared down at his cards. He clacked his false teeth dejectedly and stood up, shaking his head. "Like I tole you, Swanee, I don't got the belly for it no more."

He left the room looking more ancient and broken than ever. This time it was no act.

For the next few hands Murky got on a rush, beating Teddy Bear out of a couple nice pots, increasing his stack to about eight thousand. He was playing hard, chasing too many pots, but the cards were being good to him.

Sometime after two, Chuckie told Kingston he had to go home. "I've got the early shift at the Hand tomorrow," he said.

Kingston told Sicard to take over as dealer.

The King and I went head-to-head on a king, jack, nine flop. Me with a pair of nines. I had him figured for an ace, ten, but there was no way to be sure. He's drawing to a straight, I figured. A straight would beat my trip nines, but I didn't think he had his straight, at least not yet. I threw in a thousand, hoping to make him fold, but he smooth-called my raise.

Sicard dealt a queen.

If I was right about his hand, the King had made his straight. I checked.

He came at me with a two-thousand-dollar bet.

I took a minute to think. Three thousand in the pot, plus Kingston's bet. I'd be investing two grand to see one more card. If the last card came up a nine, a king, or a jack, I'd beat his straight—if that's what he had. There were three kings, three jacks, and one nine left in the deck. Seven winning cards out of the forty-four cards I hadn't seen. A one in six chance—assuming that I was right about his hand.

Kingston's pale gray eyes gave away nothing.

There wasn't enough money in the pot to justify the two-thousand-dollar bet. I folded.

Kingston tossed his cards faceup on the table.

Deuce, seven.

His mouth curved up in a ghastly imitation of a smile.

Rags.

I had tossed winners.

Murky laughed.

Kingston had played a bad hand just to

throw me off. Poker players call it "advertising"—bluffing with a nothing hand so that when they do get good cards, the other players will give them action. In this case, the King had won. He'd thrown me off by cold-calling my thousand-dollar raise with a nothing hand, then blew me away by topping it with a two-thousand-dollar bet when the queen fell. Like I was a fish. A rabbit. A no-talent loser.

I was furious with myself, and furious at Murky for laughing. I closed my eyes and forced my mind to clear. I gathered my emotions into a hot, tight knot, and I buried that knot deep. I felt my brain grow cold and crisp and sharp as the edges of the cards, felt my senses grow keen, felt my heartbeat slow. Sicard began to deal the next hand. The cards sailed across the table in slow motion. The sound they made when they landed on the felt was deafening. I picked up my cards. Jack, ten.

Murky laughed and bet forty.

"Raise," I said.

I won that hand, and the next. Sicard lit another cigar, his sixth since I'd arrived. I played my cards cold and hard and watched my stack grow. I busted Teddy Bear out with a pair of jacks. He stood up with a rueful smile. "I oughta stick with the slots," he said, shaking his head. "Last month I won four thousand." He dug a few quarters from his pocket and stuck them in one of the slot machines against the back wall, watching dully as the spinning cherries and oranges and plums ate up the last of his money.

"Maybe I oughta try bingo," he muttered as he made his way out the door.

That left just three of us playing, with Sicard dealing. Murky had somehow hung in there. Kingston tried to bust him twice, but both times Murky caught a lucky card on the end.

A few hands later I caught a full house on the flop. I held a pair of kings and the flop came up king, queen, queen. Only a pair of queens could beat me. I bet five hundred.

Kingston said, "Call," as he pushed forward five black chips. Murky took another look at his cards and reached for his stack.

I said, "Hey, Murk, you're up three thousand. I got you beat this hand. Why don't you quit winners for a change?"

The Murky I saw sitting across the smoke-hazed table was a Murky I didn't know. His loose grin had been replaced by a hard line. No trace of humor in his eyes. When he looked at me I could feel hatred shooting from his pupils like a spray of hot ash. I dropped my eyes to his hands. He was gripping his cards so tight his fingertips were white, his nails red and jagged, bitten down to the quick.

For a moment my knotted, buried emotions unraveled. I wanted to say, *Hey, Murk, ya wanna go over to the mall and hang out? Ya wanna go blow ten bucks in quarters at Pop's Arcade? Ya wanna go get your cane and pretend to be a blind man? Ya wanna go hang out in your bedroom and listen to CDs?*

But I couldn't say any of those things.

"My name is Mark," he said. He pushed all his chips into the pot. "And I raise."

Somewhere inside me I felt the doors slam shut. I'd done what I could.

I called his raise.

Kingston found me with his chilly eyes, then folded.

Sicard rolled the last two cards, a deuce and a jack.

Murky turned up his cards: a king, queen. He had a full house.

I showed him my kings. My full house was bigger.

I'd busted him out of the game. For his own good. Or maybe I did it because I could. Or because he'd laughed at me. The fact was, it didn't matter. I was playing it stone cold. I was no longer there to save my friend Murky. I was there to play poker.

I watched him leave, feeling nothing at all.

The King said, "Well, kid, it's just you and me."

I looked at his expressionless features and had the sudden sensation that I was staring into a distorted mirror.

I turned to Sicard and said, "Deal 'em."

I found the King's tell.

When he had a strong hand he liked to touch himself. It was subtle, but I saw him do it again and again. He would brush a finger against his chin, or touch one hand with the other, or brush an imaginary piece of lint from his lapel. Sometimes it was not an actual touch, but a gesture, a half-motion. It could mean nothing. He might have an itch, or there might actually be a piece of lint. It wasn't a great tell.

But it was enough.

Having a tell on someone is like owning a sliver of their soul. Having a tell on a man like Artie Kingston was like owning the entire man.

Kingston and I played one-on-one throughout the night. I was up twenty thousand, then forty thousand. Shortly before dawn I saw his impassive features begin to crumble. A shiny film of sweat gathered at his hairline, and a startlingly red tongue emerged to lick his lips.

Sicard said, "Mr. Kingston? You okay?"

The King nodded. "Keep dealing," he said.

He was all mine.

GRAY

So that's what happened last summer, told the way I remember it, with only a few things left out. I am sitting in my office looking out over the cold, muddy river eating *steak au poivre*, medium rare, just the way I like it. A lot of things have changed in my life, but the steaks at Marcel's are still outstanding.

I saw Murky just last week raking Mrs. Pratt's lawn. I hear he gave up gambling. I guess he decided he didn't want to be like me after all. I'm real happy for him. Too bad he hates my guts.

Kelly Rollingate is still going out with the guy from Camp Challenge. I saw them down on Front Street a couple weeks ago coming out of a movie theater. He's as tall as me, but thicker and older and hairier. If Kelly is happy with the big ape, then I'm real happy for her, too.

I'm real happy for everybody, even Fred, who went ahead and married Cindy, who is only five years older than me, his son. I got a postcard from him a few weeks back. He said he sold a script to Arnold Schwarzenegger's production company for $1.2 million. I guess he finally got what he wanted.

Fred's marriage was the final straw for my mom. Shortly thereafter, she announced that she and Big Bob were getting hitched, too. A week later they flew to Reno. Now that she's living with Big Bob she's got somebody else to open her pickle jars. They wanted me to come live with them, but I said, "No thanks." They didn't like that much. Big Bob made a lot of noise about me being a minor and so forth. He said, all red in the face, "You damn well better do as your mother says!" Instead, I hired a lawyer. That shut him up. It's amazing what you can do with money, even if you're only sixteen.

I still talk to my mom a couple times a week, but it's not the same as it used to be.

Jason Hicks is in the workhouse serving a one-year sentence. Gibby, who had a record, will be in for two years.

Seamus O'Gara ran in the New York City Marathon and finished 719th out of a field of 30,000 runners. I called to congratulate him. He was polite, but distant. He did not ask me how I was doing.

I haven't seen the King lately, not since he

handed me the keys to Marcel's, but I heard he's still in town, trying to raise a stake. I suspect he wants another crack at me. If he can raise the money, he's welcome to try.

As far as running the restaurant, Sicard takes care of everything, and all I have to do is sign checks. I hired a lawyer to keep an eye on Sicard, and another lawyer to watch the first lawyer. I don't want to be bothered with details.

I'd rather just play cards.

It's Friday night, game night. Any time now, Sicard will call to tell me he's lined up enough players. Teddy Bear will be there—he loves to play cards almost as much as I do. Potato-head will probably show up, too. His real name is Elwood Vasque, and he runs the Fairview County Health Department. I try not to let him lose too much. I haven't seen Big Bear since Kingston busted him out that night. I think he went back to St. Louis.

Cookie Green died on Halloween night. He didn't die at the poker table the way he expected. He died sitting on the toilet in the men's room at The Magic Hand. It was a heart attack, they say. Only six people showed up at his funeral—not even enough to make a decent-sized poker game. I recognized all of them from the Hand. I was surprised to learn that Cookie was only fifty-six years old.

I am waiting for the phone to ring, waiting for Sicard to call.

The setting sun is turning the silty river orange and gold. The ruins of my *steak au poivre* stare up at me from my desk, fat congealing around the edge of the plate. I feel a little nauseous from the big meal, and a little sad from thinking about Murky and Kelly and my mom and the rest of them. I wish I could think of somebody to call on the phone, but every name I think of is somebody who doesn't want to hear from me. Or somebody I'd rather not talk to.

I hear a knock at the door. It's Alfred, my headwaiter.

"Are you finished, sir?"

I nod and watch silently as he picks up my plates and glass and sets them on his tray and carries it out of my office, closing the door softly behind him.

I open my desk drawer and lift out the necklace, ninety gold beads. I pour it from one hand into the other, hearing the cool chatter of the soft, heavy, metal droplets as I watch the sunset fade from orange to gray. I am sixteen years old, going on infinity. I pour the necklace from hand to hand, feeling the metal grow warm. I own a restaurant and three cars and I am the best poker player in the state—maybe in the world. I am rich, but I don't care about the money anymore. I don't even care about being the best. All I want is to play cards, to run my fingers over those slick, hard surfaces, to feel that cold power flowing in and out through my hands and eyes.

I am waiting for the phone to ring.

One more hand.